GROUNDWORK GUIDES

Series Editor
Jane Springer

GROUNDWORK GUIDES

The Force of Law
Mariana Valverde

Groundwood Books
House of Anansi Press | Toronto Berkeley

Copyright © 2010 by Mariana Valverde
Published in Canada and the USA in 2010 by Groundwood Books

Groundwood Books / House of Anansi Press
110 Spadina Avenue, Suite 801, Toronto, Ontario M5V 2K4
or c/o Publishers Group West
1700 Fourth Street, Berkeley, CA 94710

We acknowledge for their financial support of our publishing
program the Canada Council for the Arts, the Government of Canada through
the Canada Book Fund (CBF) and the Ontario Arts Council.

Library and Archives Canada Cataloguing in Publication
Valverde, Mariana
The force of law / Mariana Valverde.
(Groundwork guides)
ISBN 978-0-88899-817-0 (bound).—ISBN 978-0-88899-818-7 (pbk.)
1. Law enforcement. 2. Law. 3. Police power. I. Title. II. Series: Groundwork guides
HV7921.V33 2010   363.2'3   C2009-906509-6

Design by Michael Solomon
Typesetting by Sari Naworynski
Index by Gillian Watts

Groundwood Books is committed to protecting our natural environment.
As part of our efforts, this book is printed on paper that contains 100%
post-consumer recycled fibers, is acid-free and is processed chlorine-free.

Printed and bound in Canada

Contents

This book is dedicated to Nicolas, Ming, José Luis, Laura, Carolina and Kevin — in the hope that their generation will do a better job of working towards justice.

Chapter 1
What Is the Law?

What is the law? And why does it matter so much?

People talk about "law" in two quite different senses. Citizens often argue about whether specific laws are good or bad — as in public debates about whether marijuana should be legalized or whether women's access to abortion should or should not be subject to legal limits. The specific laws that are in effect in a particular country at a particular time make up "the law," in the sense of laws that actually exist.

But "the law" is also a term with a broader and loftier meaning. For centuries now, many people around the world have fought hard, even giving up their lives, for the sake of defending the rule of law in their country. In nineteenth-century Europe there were revolutions in France, in Germany, in Spain and in other countries that tried to replace the arbitrary rule of monarchs by a system in which no one would be above the law. More recently, the hundreds of lawyers and judges who risked their careers and their physical safety by participating in a street demonstration in Pakistan, in June

2008, to demand the reinstatement of Chief Justice Iftikhar Chaudhry and about sixty other judges summarily deposed by the president were not marching for or against a particular law. They were putting their lives on the line to defend lawfulness as such.

Specific laws come and go, and few citizens are willing to go to the wall to either defend or oppose a particular law. But law in general, the rule of law, is absolutely crucial. What does the phrase "the rule of law" mean?

The principles of the rule of law developed over time, as citizens became unhappy with being loyal subjects of absolute monarchs and undertook the tremendous task of devising forms of government that would be accountable to the people. Accountability is at the heart of the idea of the rule of law. Accountability (also known as "responsibility") is a key political principle, much older than the right to vote, by which governments are obligated to act in the public interest and to give a satisfactory account of their actions and policies to their people.

Accountability and democracy are not the same thing. Indeed, the rule of law is not identified with any one system of government. Britain is still a monarchy, while most other advanced industrial countries are republics (or states without monarchs). Some countries have parliamentary governments that can fall if a few small parties organize a coalition against the ruling party; other systems are presidential, and rely on citizens directly electing their president at set times. But even though the most populous country in the world is ruled by a collective dictator (the central committee of the Communist Party of China), by and large, there is a great deal of agreement amongst the citizens of the world — including millions of Chinese citizens — on the principles of the rule of law, and accountability is a key such principle.

"The rule of law" also implies that rulers and government officials are all subject to the same laws as citizens — that is, nobody is above the law. When the Pakistani lawyers took to the streets, they did so because the president wanted to change the constitution so that he could serve a third term, and he knew the Pakistani high court would not approve this. Standing up for the fired chief justice was thus standing up for the principle that no person, even if elected president, can manipulate the legal system for his or her own benefit.

A closely related principle of the rule of law is that everyone is entitled to what US law calls "the equal protection of the law." In other words, laws have to be applicable to everyone and be administered fairly, without favoring particular groups or individuals. When African Americans fought in the 1950s and 1960s against segregation, technically, they were fighting for equal protection. A school district that consigned black children to inferior, separate schools was a breach of the rule of law, it was argued, even if state legislatures had put the system in place by passing laws. The lawyers' arguments had to try to find some text in the American Constitution to use as a weapon in the court cases. This was not easy since the Constitution had been ratified at a time when slavery was perfectly legal. But by using the same principles of fairness and accountability that people in other countries were using to attack unjust political and legal systems, they were able to persuade a sufficient number of judges and legislators that "equal protection" did not mean treating all African Americans equally, but rather treating all Americans equally. The basic principle here was fairness.

Fairness usually involves treating everyone equally, but sometimes fairness requires taking different needs and different resources into consideration. For example, income taxes are fairer than flat, arithmetically equal per-head taxes.

Together, accountability, fairness and the principle that nobody is above the law since the law applies to all equally make up the core of the rule of law. Citizens opposing government abuses of power care enough about the rule of law to put their bodies on the line for these seemingly abstract principles. From Alabama in the 1960s to Pakistan and Tibet in 2008, citizens really do care about the rule of law. And governments everywhere live in fear of being criticized by Amnesty International and other non-governmental organizations for human rights abuses and other breaches of the principles of law.

Why does the rule of law matter so much to so many people? It matters in part because injustice and oppression are all too common, all too visible, and most people know we need to be vigilant to oppose them or prevent their return. Even citizens of stable democracies, people who have not had to fight personally to establish accountable governments, can read in their history books about the dreadful injustices committed by their governments in the not-so-distant past—the genocide of aboriginal peoples in North America, for example, or the injustices wreaked on Africans and Asians by European colonial powers, with legal impunity, up until the 1960s.

But the rule of law also matters at a more personal, emotional level. Utopianism is not in fashion in the twenty-first century, but most people are moved not only by a dislike of nasty injustices but by a positive vision of just communities. We often experience fairness, accountability and justice only on a micro-scale — in a community group, in dealing with a government official who turns out to be surprisingly fair, or in other very small settings. But while citizens everywhere are skeptical about politicians and governments, law as such, the principles of law, still command not just respect but passion. Soldiers who are sent on peacekeeping missions do not die for any government. They die for the principles of fairness and accountability. Citizens who spend thousands of volunteer hours fighting to obtain laws that will preserve the environment are not fighting just for one specific law. They are fighting to make governments accountable to their people and for the broader principle of our responsibility to nature and to future generations.

That laws matter a great deal is fairly obvious, if only because all of us have to deal with parking tickets, misleading contracts, legal obligations to pay taxes, unpleasant officials, and any number of other embodiments of the laws of our country on an everyday basis. Each day every citizen living in a market economy interacts with law dozens of times. But few of these laws really go to the heart of what it is to live in a community. In the end, the citizens of the world care more about the rule of law than about particular laws — and rightly so. There are many crises that demand attention in today's world, and all of them require some kind of law, some legal tools. From global climate change to the persistence of racial inequality, none of the world's pressing problems will be adequately addressed unless governments are held accountable to their citizens by their citizens, and are made to pass laws that treat everyone — including future generations — fairly.

If we move from this consideration of laws and the rule of law to the other part of the book's title — the "force" in "the force of law" — the first thing to note is that laws do not interpret or enforce themselves. The law of gravity enforces itself, but the criminal law does not. Every legal system needs human beings to enforce it. Enforcement is often a quiet and informal process that uses social and peer pressure to get people to behave properly (what sociologists call "informal social control"). But while most people are law-abiding out of habit, out of duty, or out of fear of disapproval, law sometimes requires specialized personnel who are authorized to use coercion (or the use of force or threats) and even violence to enforce the law.

This highlights the crucial paradox of the book's title.

While law is usually regarded as the civilized, nonviolent way to deal with harms and conflicts, violence is integral to law. Police are, after all, allowed to handcuff, manhandle, Taser and even sometimes kill people, and courts of law can and do confine people to prison and even, in some jurisdictions, order that they be killed. Talking about law in general is a pleasant philosophical pursuit. But many of the legal problems and issues that concern ordinary citizens have to do not with what law says or with the niceties of definitions of law, but with how laws are enforced, against whom and with what effects.

Law is not always subject to enforcement by officials such as police or immigration officers. International law is the area of law that is most fraught with enforcement difficulties. International law emerged as that special body of legal principles that governs relations among sovereign states, just as ordinary domestic (or national) law regulates relations between citizens of the same country and between the government and the citizenry. In recent years international law has been called on to attempt to indict dictators who threaten their own people, but so far it has been unsuccessful. For example, in March 2009 the International Criminal Court issued an arrest warrant for Sudan's Omar al-Bashir for war crimes and crimes against humanity against the people of Darfur, in the west of Sudan, but he continues to govern. Just how international law can be used by one country or one group of countries to intervene in the internal affairs of a far-away nation is not at all clear. What is clear is that there is little point in having international agreements and UN conventions on basic rights if there is no enforcement mechanism. As the seventeenth-century English legal theorist Thomas Hobbes famously put it, "Covenants without the sword are but words." Enforcement, then, which may involve violence, is an integral part of law.

The fact that coercion and violence are integral to law itself is often ignored by lawyers and judges, many of whom idealize the law and believe that it is the opposite of brute force. The idealization ignores not only the violence inherent in law enforcement but the fact that in most cases, a country's revered constitution arose out of violent confrontations, civil wars, revolutions and conquests. The great German philosopher Walter Benjamin, in his "Theses on the Philosophy of History" (written in the late 1930s), said that law is made up of two kinds of violence: the violence that founds law (a revolution against a colonial power, for example) and the violence that perpetuates law (the everyday violence of law enforcement).[1] In keeping with this insight, this book examines the many, often hidden connections between force and law.

If law has often been wrongly imagined to be the opposite of force or violence, Western law has also been thought of as the opposite of custom or tradition. During the glory days of the British Empire, for instance, British officials and missionaries believed that Africans and Asians were far too caught up in their traditional customs, and that a good modern legal system would greatly improve the situation in those countries. They assumed that the rules that governed social interactions among "natives" were not laws because they were not written down, or because there was no specialized body of officials charged with enforcing laws. It was taken for granted, until well into the twentieth century, that aboriginal peoples had customs and traditions, whereas Europeans had laws.

For a long time this simplistic way of dividing things up went unquestioned. But as the twentieth century wore on and colonialism came under question, the colonial assumptions about law also came under question. Some people from the Global South began to ask, why are elders not their community's judges? Why is it better to have full-time specially trained judges than the wisdom of ordinary people? And why is it necessary for laws to be written down?

It is clear that law consists of far more than the systems of rules that Europeans happen to prefer. Scholars and activists alike, in countries from South Africa to Australia to Canada, are having farsighted discussions about aboriginal law — a phrase that nineteenth-century colonial officials would have dismissed as an oxymoron. It has also become clear that much of what counts as law in the Western world is full of Eurocentric and moralistic prejudices. This book provides a global, less Eurocentric perspective on law and law enforcement.

Including questions of law enforcement and policing within a discussion of law, the book also aims to dispel the myth that law is one thing and violence is another. Law enforcement is coercive and sometimes even violent, which makes it seem as if it's the opposite of rational law. But enforcement is an integral and necessary part of law. This needs to be widely understood. Law is too important to be left to lawyers, and law enforcement is too important to be left to the police. Citizens who care about justice and democracy need to be knowledgeable both about the laws they live under and about how these laws are enforced.

Chapter 2
Kafka's Challenge

One of the most evocative novels about law of all time, Franz Kafka's *The Trial*, begins with the protagonist, Josef K, being awakened by some unidentifiable officers who have come to arrest him.[1] Josef protests, "And why am I under arrest?" The officers reply, "We don't answer questions like that." They explain that they are lowly employees, mere cogs in a wheel, and that he will have to accompany them and then wait to see what the charges are. Josef repeats that he has not done anything wrong and frantically searches for identity documents to prove he is a law-abiding citizen. Playing upon the guilt feelings that we all tend to experience when questioned by authorities, one of the arresting officers tells Josef, "Our authorities as far as I know, and I only know the lowest grade, don't go out looking for guilt among the public; it's the guilt that draws them out, like it says in the law, and they have to send us police officers out." Josef wonders about this mysterious, all-seeing law. "I don't know this law," he says.[2]

At that point the officials have Josef K where they want him. He has admitted that he doesn't know all of the laws, which means he cannot possibly be certain that he hasn't broken any. "So much the worse for you, then," they say. And one says to the other, "Look at this, Willem: he admits he doesn't know the law and at the same time insists he's innocent."

Since ignorance of the law is not a valid excuse in a criminal trial, all of us could potentially find ourselves in Josef K's shoes. And in fact, our situation in regard to the law is uncannily like that of Josef K. Like him we could be unknowingly breaching laws we don't know, but even in the case of laws we do happen to know, we cannot really always know whether we're on the right side of the law.

Even small children know that stealing is against the law. But it is not always easy to know what stealing is. What about a situation in which someone regularly borrows a neighbor's lawn mower, with permission, but one day borrows it for what the neighbor considers to be an overly long period of time? Or what about someone who pockets a twenty-dollar bill found on the sidewalk? It turns out that pocketing the bill is not stealing — under English and North American law at any rate. "Finders keepers" is not just a children's rhyme. It is a legal maxim. The lawn mower situation, for its part, is a gray area. If the dispute went to court, a judge would have to listen carefully to the neighbors' accounts of their intentions and their actions before making a decision.

We can never be sure that we are actually law-abiding. Even those of us living in established democracies with police forces that are not particularly corrupt are still subject to regular harassment by any number of Kafkaesque authorities who may turn out to have the letter of the law on their side, however irrational or unfair their demands may seem. We may know for a fact that there was no sign posted stating this bit of road is a no-parking zone. Or we may be certain that a sum of money we received did not need to be declared on our income tax form or divulged to the social worker who monitors our social security payments. But when facing an official who claims that we are in breach of the law, we may feel not only powerless but also anxious and unsure. As Kafka famously showed, it is impossible to prove that the law is on our side.

Part of the reason for this constant threat of finding oneself on the wrong side of the law is the simple fact that law is enforced by human beings. Human action is necessarily affected by prejudices, laziness, ignorance, self-interest, bad moods and other sources of arbitrariness. But the problem would not be solved by having computerized systems take care of law enforcement. Along with the numerous sources of human error, a key factor underlying the essential uncertainty of law and law enforcement is that human life is far too complicated to be properly slotted into law's pigeonholes. One can pass laws against stealing, but one can never set down in advance rules that are so fine-tuned that they would leave no uncertainty about the legal status of borrowing the neighbor's lawn mower.

Although applying general rules and principles to specific situations will always involve subjective judgments, the basic principles of legality are, on the whole, well established. It is ironic that these basic principles are better known to citizens of countries with bad human rights records and undemocratic governments than they are to citizens of democracies. The reason for this is that the principles — collectively known as the rule of law — become more visible and more important when people are keenly aware that they cannot take them for granted. For instance, in Latin American countries that suffered for years under tyrannical military governments, the principle that subordinates armies to civilian politicians is discussed in everyday life as well as in formal speeches. In the US, Britain and France, by contrast, citizens rarely stop to think about the fact that it is politicians, not generals, who decide whether to send troops to Iraq or Afghanistan. It is thus worthwhile to go over some of the basic principles that can never remove the essential uncertainty of law, but which try to ensure that governments themselves — the makers of laws — also follow the rules and laws that bind citizens.

The Rule of Law

In the English-speaking world the idea of the rule of law is usually traced back to the medieval Magna Carta, although that famous document was concerned with limiting the king's power over barons, not with the welfare or the rights of all subjects of the king. After the English

Magna Carta

Many English people believe that the principles of accountable and fair government known as the rule of law were invented in medieval England and enshrined in the Magna Carta, a thirteenth-century document that powerful barons and bishops pressured King John to sign. The document (available on the British Library website)[3] sets out some key principles of governmental fairness, especially in regard to the justice system:

> (39) No free man shall be seized or imprisoned, or stripped of his rights or possessions, or outlawed or exiled... except by the lawful judgment of his equals or by the law of the land.

> (40) To no one will we [the king] sell, to no one deny or delay right or justice.

However, most of the sixty-three clauses of the Magna Carta concern the privileges, power and wealth of "free men" — not including women or serfs — and more specifically, of barons and bishops. Clause 61 illustrates the feudal bias of the document:

> Since we [the king] have granted all these things for God, for the better ordering of our kingdom, and to allay the discord that has arisen between us and our barons, and since we desire that they shall be enjoyed in their entirety, with lasting strength, forever, we give and grant to the barons the following security: the barons shall elect twenty-five of their number to keep, and cause to be observed with all their might, the peace and liberties granted and confirmed to them by this charter.

Revolution of the late 1600s and the French Revolution of 1789, government power in most of Europe and in North America shifted to representative bodies — that is, legislatures. Monarchs had typically ruled through edicts and decrees — rules dictated by an all-powerful monarch or minister — often targeting specific situations, groups or even individuals. Kings could make pronouncements regarding the fate of Protestants or of Jews as a group. They could also seize the property of aristocrats who challenged their power, and they could put in place rules restricting economic activity, either for a particular industry or in a specific town or port.

As monarchs were either totally replaced by a representative government (as in France and the US) or demoted to the position of formal heads of state (as in Britain), the legislative work of parliaments and similar representative bodies grew in importance. The idea was that citizens ought to know in advance what was legal or illegal instead of being subjected to retroactive rules. And rules were to be of general application, not targeted to favor a particular faction or business interest or to persecute a particular group. Furthermore, these rules ought to be debated by the people's representatives and set down in publicly proclaimed laws (or statutes).

The most enduring of these law reform projects was the Napoleonic Code — rather ironically, given that Napoleon seized power within France by force and imposed it on other European countries by military might. But despite its undemocratic origins, this code is the basis of the current legal systems of a large number of countries. The influence of the Napoleonic Code extends not only across Europe and parts of Africa but throughout Latin America. As the former Spanish Empire crumbled, in the early 1800s, republican governments arose that were inspired by the American Revolution, the French Revolution and, more generally, popular movements that sought to either limit royal power or replace it altogether. The Napoleonic Code was the key source of post-monarchical law outside the English-speaking world.

While different legal traditions cite different sources for the rule of law, in general, in today's world, a "government of laws and not of men" means that nobody is above the law, even kings and presidents and prime ministers. (John Adams, second president of the US, included this phrase in the Massachusetts Constitution in 1780.) This is why kickbacks and bribes are regarded as extremely serious political sins, even if the amounts are not large and even if it is not clear that the business interests doing the bribing actually got the expected benefits. Governments are supposed to work according to general rules that treat everyone equally: anything that gives particular citizens undue influence is a breach not only of particular statutes and rules governing politicians and bureaucrats but of the basic principles of the rule of law.

In Britain Prime Minister Tony Blair's last years in office (2006-2007) were marred by an inquiry into influence peddling in the conferring of peerages. Allegations that certain people were appointed as lords because they gave the ruling Labour Party loans on favorable terms were regarded as serious breaches of the rule of law. The individuals involved had not actually bribed anyone, but provided loans on better terms than those offered by banks. Despite the fact that the conduct in question was not criminal, the inquiry, which saw a sitting prime minister questioned in regard to breaches of the electoral funding rules and the customary principles governing peerage appointments, was regarded by many as warranting his resignation.

This scandal highlights the irony that while Britain sees itself as having invented the rule of law, it is also the country that has most successfully preserved pre-democratic institutions: a state-approved church (the Church of England), an inherited monarchy and a House of Lords. The House of Lords has always been an unelected legislative body made up precisely of those individuals who either personally or through inheritance are much more powerful and wealthy than their fellow citizens. Other democracies have "upper houses" (usually called senates), but none has a legislative body made up largely of the super-rich and of the descendants of old aristocrats. It is difficult to reconcile the very existence of the House of Lords with the principles of the rule of law. Perhaps because of this, it is deemed politically essential to maintain the appearance of impartiality in appointments of new Lords. Tony Blair's government had some years earlier abolished the hereditary peerage, maintaining that in a modern state operating under the rule of law there was no place for legislators whose only qualification was being born to a peer. The scandal about party funding demonstrated that having peers appointed by the government of the day is not necessarily better, from the point of view of the rule of law, than the hereditary system.

Despite the persistence of both formal (e.g., the House of Lords) and informal avenues through which powerful interests pressure governments to obtain favorable rules, a crucial element of statutes passed by assemblies is that they should be of general application, meaning they apply equally to everyone. Legislatures to this day still sometimes pass laws affecting only a small piece of territory or a particular corporation, but a key component of the rule-of-law system is that the vast majority of laws apply to everyone. Thus, if a legislature passes a law raising the sales tax, for example, it might be possible to create an exception for certain products deemed to be essential necessities rather than optional purchases. But it would be a breach of the rule of law to exempt Mr FatCat's products from tax laws, as was routinely done in the days of absolute monarchies.

The Law of Laws

Principles such as equality before the law are crucial elements of the rule of law. But in addition, in most countries, there is a key structure that ensures a government of laws and not of men — the constitution. A constitution is best described as the law of laws. The object of a constitution is to ensure that neither politicians nor bureaucrats issue rules and decisions that exceed their powers or contravene the basic rules of the political game. Particular laws passed by parliament, or rules put in place by presidents or ministers, need to keep within the boundaries set by the constitution. The bodies that decide whether or not a law or rule is constitutional are supreme courts or special constitutional courts.

The most important exception to this system is Britain. There is a British constitution, but it remains an unwritten set of principles that have been elaborated in numerous judicial decisions that are not gathered systematically in a single published text.

In the United States, which is regarded internationally as having pioneered the idea of constitutional government, much of the constitutional work of the Supreme Court is devoted to drawing the lines separating municipal, state and federal governmental action. For example, if a municipality headed by a "green" mayor decided to place a heavy tax on over-packaged goods, it is likely that a court would rule this action *ultra vires* (a Latin phrase meaning "outside of its powers") because rules governing commerce are part of the state's power, not municipal power. This may seem to be a purely technical issue. But given the centuries-long struggles to limit royal power, the legal question of jurisdiction is of more than legalistic interest. When one level of government infringes on the powers of another level of government, the basic rules of the game are being breached.

Besides outlining the respective powers of different branches of government and different levels, constitutions also protect the rights of citizens against government interference. In this regard, the US Constitution has often served as a model for other countries, since it enshrined such rights as free speech earlier and in a more powerful form than any other state. But the constitutional rights of citizens against states don't necessarily make up the bulk of constitutional courts' work. Citizens' individual rights may be what most people know about their particular constitution, but constitutional courts probably spend less time on individual rights than on the work of ensuring that the division of powers between different branches and levels of government is maintained.

Because a constitution serves as the law of laws, there are usually many barriers preventing sitting governments from changing it. These barriers involve elaborate processes for constitutional amendments and the need for agreement by a super-majority (i.e., a vote by two-thirds or three-fifths of those voting rather than a simple 51 percent majority). In general, one of the principles of the rule of law is that constitutions ought not to be changed every time there is a change in government, since the constitution of a country is meant to embody the most fundamental, almost sacred principles of government.

Statute Law and Common Law

In most of the world, the principles of the rule of law and representative government require that judges limit themselves to applying laws. Proper law is written law; proper law is the product of legislatures. Proper law, in other words, is made up of statutes. A judge presiding over a trial has to establish whether Ms Sleazy's conduct falls within the parameters of a published legal rule established by a legislature, say the rule defining "corruption." If the evidence suggests that Ms Sleazy did indeed hand over an envelope containing cash to a ministry official charged with making decisions affecting Ms Sleazy's construction business, and that particular activity seems to be covered by the wording of the corruption statute, then Ms Sleazy is found guilty. The judge's activity consists in reading the statute carefully and seeing whether the conduct that has been shown to have taken place falls within the pigeonhole provided by the statute. Systems in which the judge's role is solely to interpret and apply statutes are known as civil-law jurisdictions.

In Britain and its former colonies, however, the law does not consist only of statutes. There is also a large body of law known as the common law. This consists of the accumulation of judicial decisions — or, more particularly, those decisions that have been noticed subsequently and have not been overturned by later or higher courts.

Before computer databases, studying the common law involved reading hundreds of published decisions dating back centuries — but doing so in the knowledge that any of these could be overturned in the brief time between having studied them and beginning to practice law. Nowadays, learning cases is easier. Legal databases are updated daily to add a red flag to decisions that have been overturned, while search functions allow students and lawyers to find out quickly whether a judicial decision, or even just one tiny bit of the decision, has been subsequently discussed, and if so, by what level of court.

Nevertheless, learning and applying the law remain very challenging in common-law countries. In civil-law countries, where law simply means statutes, young people can become judges just as they become tax inspectors, through a civil service exam that one can take straight out of university, whereas in common-law countries judges are appointed from a pool of experienced lawyers. The difficulty does not lie only in the vast volume of judicial decisions that need to be taken into account by common-law courts, but in the fact that common-law courts rarely issue general pronouncements. Previous judicial decisions that a lawyer might wish to cite are always somewhat dependent on and constrained by the particular facts of those cases.

For example, a ruling granting custody of little Susie and little Jake to Ms X and occasional access to her estranged husband Mr X has to be grounded in legal principles. It cannot be driven by the judge's personal feelings about the relative merits and faults of the parents. However, while principles and previous important judicial decisions (or precedents) will certainly be cited in the judge's ruling, much attention will also be paid to specific circumstances, such as how much time each parent generally spent looking after the children, how decisions were made regarding schooling and other matters, and the opinions of psychologists and other experts. This means that subsequent courts may find it difficult to determine, when reading the judge's decision, whether the key factor was really that Ms X is gainfully employed and Mr X is not, or whether the decision is mainly a reflection of established societal views about young children's well-being depending more on mothers than fathers. Even if the judge explicitly mentioned Ms X's steady income, and did not mention motherhood or gender, the decision may be sidelined in a later case in which a father with a good job is trying to obtain custody.

This illustrates a general problem of the common law. In written decisions in which judgments are made about people's conduct or about the credibility of a particular witness, it is impossible for even the most self-aware judges to know what weight different factors had in the complex process by which a decision is reached. Given that judges are rarely, if ever, representative of the population, systemic biases are bound to affect the process. Unconsciously held ideas about what is proper and reasonable cannot be wholly eliminated or even made explicit. Feminist legal scholarship has shown that views about gender and family relations deriving from religion or from custom play a large role in law, even when — or perhaps especially when — the judge in question is not consciously thinking about gender issues.

A sense of the depth of the problem can be gained by looking at the 1980s debate in Canada and the US about whether battered women who killed their abusers could plead self-defense even if the homicide took place when the woman was not actually being attacked. At issue in these cases was the traditional legal test by which conduct is evaluated by comparing it to what the "reasonable man" (a key building block of the common law) would do in the circumstances. Feminist lawyers argued that traditional legal standards did not apply to women who had been belittled and abused for years, women who felt that their abusers would pursue them and possibly kill them if they fled from the home, and who therefore chose to kill the abuser while he was asleep or otherwise not directly threatening them. Traditionally law would consider such an action premeditated murder. The argument for self-defense, in contrast, is conventionally applied in bar-fight situations or other struggles involving two people who do not have a complicated intimate relationship of inequality and domination.

In order to change the legal standard that had been required to obtain a not-guilty verdict by reason of self-defense, feminist lawyers argued that battered wives generally feel too powerless to move out or otherwise escape, and that therefore they ought not to be judged by the same standards applied in male-male bar fights. This argument went to the heart of the concept of the "reasonable man." Some courts in Canada and in the US ended up agreeing with the feminist argument that what is or is not a reasonable act of self-defense may depend on gender-specific factors, and that the "reasonable man" standard was indeed a man's standard, in need of being replaced by a more flexible "reasonable person" standard. This challenged a basic assumption of the rule of law, namely, that everyone regardless of gender, race and culture ought to be evaluated by exactly the same legal rules.

The feminist challenge to the law's idea of equality — an idea that would quickly conclude that the battered woman who killed her husband while he was asleep was nothing but a murderer — has not been definitively settled. Indeed, it has been complicated by questions arising from cultural difference. In other cases, often also involving violence against women, defense lawyers argued that men belonging to certain cultural groups could be regarded as acting "reasonably" if they sought to prevent their daughters from socializing with or marrying whomever they want. Some lawyers also argued that men of certain cultural groups could not be expected to remain cool and rational if they discovered that their wives or daughters were contravening traditional morality. This was known as "the cultural defense." The cultural defense has rarely been successful in courts. But it is important to note that the very meaning of the basic principle of equality before the law is under negotiation in a debate that is unlikely to be conclusively resolved.

Gender, race and culture continue to be factors in the negotiation of basic legal concepts and standards. But an additional, less political factor underlying the inherent uncertainty of law, especially in English-speaking countries using the common law, is that in any area of law there are bound to be a number of potential precedents or authoritative earlier decisions that are relevant to a legal dispute.

Uncertainty is also a feature of statute law and civil law, since one can usually argue about whether the words of the statute do or do not cover the facts of the current case. But the common law is more in a state of flux than civil law. There is much more to argue about when instead of one or two statutes setting out general rules, lawyers have an indeterminate number of earlier cases to draw upon. It is often difficult to tell how similar the facts of a subsequent case have to be before the earlier decision counts as a precedent.

To add to the complications of the common law, precedents don't all have the same status. A higher appeal court will always be more authoritative than a lower court, but lower courts often disagree amongst themselves, and many of these disagreements are never sorted out by a higher court. In the US, for example, a decision of the federal Supreme Court will always trump decisions of lower state courts, but it is far less clear whether a decision from one state will be found to be a proper precedent in a case being heard in a different state.

In exceptional instances decisions from other countries may be used as precedents. In the US, after the revolution, English judicial decisions continued to be treated as authoritative. Nowadays, most high courts in the common-law world recognize each other as authoritative, at least in cases in which the country's own law is in flux. The Israeli Supreme Court, for example, regularly cites Canadian Supreme Court precedents. The US, by contrast, has tended to narrow the scope of what can be used as authoritative precedent, to the dismay of human rights lawyers trying to use international law or foreign law, for example, to influence American refugee law or to help the structure, fence, sign, seat, bench or ornament of any kind or in any way foul or pollute any fountain, lake, stream, pool, pond, well or spring in any park, or injure, deface or destroy any notices, rules or regulations posted or affixed to anything by order or permission of the [Park] Board.

7. No person shall play at any game whatsoever in any portion of any park except upon or in such portions thereof as may be especially allotted, designed and provided, respectively, for any purpose, and under such rules and regulations and at such times as shall be prescribed by the Board, and without limiting the generality of the foregoing, no person shall:

  a) play golf or strike a golf ball;
  b) fly any motor-driven model airplane;
  c) shoot any arrow or practice archery;
  d) take part in any ball game;
  e) use a skateboard, roller skates, ice skates, or any similar device;

except in areas designated or permitted for such activities.

prisoners in Guantanamo Bay, Cuba (where the US has held hundreds of foreigners deemed to be "terrorists" since October 2001).

Occasionally, foreign law is considered authoritative even in the US. In the 2003 Supreme Judicial Court of Massachusetts decision legalizing same-sex marriage in that state, Canadian case law was cited as the main precedent. This upset many, because most American courts and lawyers seem convinced that American law is influential elsewhere but is not itself subject to foreign influence. Given that — like Canadian law — American law arose out of English law and used much of English common law long after statutes and constitutions had been produced, it is a bit difficult for US courts to maintain that only American precedents count.

The common law, therefore, is inevitably political. Civil-law systems allow judges some room to maneuver due to the inherent difficulties of applying general rules to specific situations. But when battles can be mounted not only about what a text means but about which texts should be considered when making a decision, the opportunities for fights featuring political convictions as well as legal disagreements expand.

This does not mean that law is nothing but politics. In most democratic countries in which the judicial branch is independent of the government of the day, judges are genuinely committed to following legal rules even when these rules produce results they find politically or morally distasteful. Courts sometimes become heavily politicized (a recent example is the morally conservative judges appointed to the US Supreme Court by President Reagan and President George W. Bush). But the ideals about impartial judges applying fair laws to everyone equally are not completely hollow. Indeed, in a large number of countries ordinary citizens may feel more fairly treated by the courts than by the government bureaucracy. Even in China, a country that does not claim to be democratic and does not have a Western-style legal system, ordinary citizens, who do not have the right to choose among competing political parties, are now beginning to take their government to court to fight against evictions and expropriations. Law is often driven by political and economic interests, but that does not mean the legal system cannot be used by citizens to win some battles against established interests.

Chapter 3
Law and Culture, Law and Justice

In China people are expected to eat with chopsticks. In Europe people are expected to eat with knives and forks, but there are many exceptions to this rule — everyone knows that some foods (e.g., apples, chocolate and bread) can be eaten with one's hands. And in China, restaurants usually serve the soup course last, whereas European restaurants invariably serve soup first.

Dining etiquette is not enshrined in any legal code, but in many ways it functions as if it were part of a state's law. Parents spend a huge amount of time teaching children table manners, and any restaurant waiter or patron who does not follow the local rules about what one eats when and how is likely to receive worse looks than if she or he were caught committing a minor infraction of the law.

Anthropologists have long documented the astounding variety of cultural differences in "norms," that is, non-legal rules governing everyday conduct. Most of these rules are so ingrained that we don't realize we are following rules until we travel abroad and suddenly see ordinary, unremarkable behavior as rule-governed behavior. How people line up to wait for a bus; how people distribute themselves in a space crowded with strangers, such as an elevator or a subway car; how people express feelings such as sexual attraction or disapproval — everyday life is made up of situations in which we don't begin from scratch to make decisions about what to do. Without anyone holding a gun to our heads, we follow established cultural patterns that we have learned to accept as "the way things are done" and that set out the rules of conduct with more effectiveness than most legal codes.

Anthropological studies of the norms governing everyday life have in recent years been used to help us better understand how law works. A consistent finding is that laws that express or embody strong social norms are treated very seriously, and citizens are upset if this kind of lawbreaker is not punished, whereas laws that don't have the cultural weight of norms behind them can often be ignored with impunity. Take, for example, the recent marked changes in public smoking in many countries around the world. (Some 80 of the world's 195 countries, or about 41 percent, prohibit smoking in some public places.) In the 1960s, medical evidence regarding the evils of cigarette smoking was available, but if medical authorities had succeeded in getting politicians to ban smoking from offices, airports and restaurants, there is no doubt that the vast majority of the population of these countries would have flouted the law. Smoking was then completely acceptable. In the 1990s, laws and regulations were put in place greatly restricting or even prohibiting smoking in indoor public spaces. By then social norms had changed so drastically that state authorities could count on citizens to participate actively in their own policing and to complain about any establishment that did not follow the letter of the no-smoking law.

Smoking laws are of course not followed to the letter. But what is surprising, given the addictive properties of cigarettes, is that they are followed as much as they are, despite the scarcity of uniformed personnel devoted to enforcing such rules. Highly restrictive laws limiting smoking have only worked because they followed a major change in social norms.

By contrast, when the US government passed a law completely banning the sale of alcoholic beverages in 1919, a significant temperance movement had not managed to truly change the social norms. While few people spoke up in public to defend the sale of liquor, vast numbers of people quietly broke the law, continuing to drink "bootleg" liquor in their homes and in speakeasies (illegal bars). Politicians realized that a forceful law that does not have social norms behind it causes more problems than it solves. Laws that are seriously out of sync with social norms are not regarded as real laws, and the disregard in which they are held may end up affecting people's attitudes toward law in general.

In some countries, few people actually pay the income tax they are supposed to pay, because they regard the state as corrupt and beholden to private interests. In many other liberal democratic countries, there are certainly many who cheat on income tax. In some other countries people might indeed cheat but they are less likely to do so, not because they have a greater likelihood of being caught and punished, but because they feel guilty about tax avoidance.

The relation between social norms and the law becomes particularly thorny in the case of societies in which different groups with somewhat different sets of norms live side by side but still have to come up with laws of general application. In the early years of the twenty-first century, France saw a protracted debate about a new law that prohibited Muslim head coverings in state schools. (The law does not specifically mention either Muslims or scarves. It is written in a neutral manner so as to target all religious symbols. But it is Muslim girls and women who feel targeted and who have been the object of law enforcement.) In Canada, a country that explicitly embraces "multiculturalism," courts would immediately strike down any such law as unconstitutional, a breach of the basic human rights of freedom of religion and freedom of expression. In France, however, where education authorities fought long and hard to eliminate the Catholic Church from its monopoly position in the school system in the late nineteenth century, many people feel that to allow any religious group to express itself, however quietly, in a state institution, is to threaten the very fabric of the secular, universalist republic that believes in *égalité*.

What this controversy shows is that in France there is a different theory of the relation between law and norms than there is in Canada. In Canada men who follow the Sikh religion and are obligated by their religious norms to keep their hair uncut and wrapped in a turban are allowed to join the national police force, the Royal Canadian Mounted Police (RCMP), and wear a turban instead of the official Mountie hat. Norms that express religious values are thus regarded as compatible with state there was a policy to never prosecute heterosexual couples engaging in "non-standard" sex. This would have been a fatal flaw in many courts in other countries, but the US Supreme Court ruled that "homosexual sodomy," even if committed in strict privacy, could be made a crime by any state that so chose. (Many states had long repealed their sodomy laws.)

In 2003, in *Lawrence v. Texas*, a case involving an interracial gay male couple, the US Supreme Court finally recognized that prevalent norms did not warrant persecuting a minority group (homosexuals) to the extent of punishing them for activities carried out in strict privacy. Justice Kennedy stated: "When homosexual conduct is made criminal by the law of the state, that declaration in and of itself is an invitation to subject homosexual persons to discrimination both in the public and in the private sphere."

Striking down sodomy laws did not, however, confer any positive rights to be free from discrimination. Gays could still be fired from certain jobs, and states were free to pass new laws (the Defense of Marriage acts or DOMA) explicitly denying recognition to couples who had married in jurisdictions allowing gay marriage. This was in contravention of the general legal principle that a person who is legally married in one country or state is recognized as married elsewhere. Striking down sodomy laws as unconstitutional has not brought about equal rights for American gays and lesbians.

law, even in the symbolically important institution of the RCMP. Indeed, in Canada, the state often facilitates and funds the expression of culturally specific norms (e.g., providing "heritage" language education in schools with many immigrant students). France, by contrast, is a state that has since the Revolution of 1789 considered principles of law as such to be at odds with the expression of cultural norms. The principles of universality, impartiality and formal equality are embodied in secular republican rituals that leave no room for religious or culturally specific norms.

Laws and Customs

The complicated relation between law and culture, discussed above by looking at laws versus norms, can also be explored from the point of view of the distinction between law and custom. The writers and activists who elaborated the key concepts of legal modernity—rights of man, constitutions, the rule of law—in the second half of the eighteenth century were all avid readers of travel tales and amateur anthropology. Sometimes they even pretended to take the standpoint of an "oriental" traveler in Europe to show up the ridiculousness of much European law and many European norms (as was famously done in Montesquieu's *Lettres Persanes*). But while they used more or less fictional tales about travelers from the East or "noble savages" from the Americas to hone their critiques of absolute monarchies and aristocratic values and norms, it did not occur to them that "orientals" and "savages" might have legal systems of their own. For Europeans — including those who went off to settle North America and various other colonies — law as such was a purely Western thing. Savages did not have laws. They had customs.

China and India, countries with extremely long and philosophically complex literate traditions, posed a bit of a problem for this Eurocentric dichotomy opposing law to custom. In the case of India it was possible to argue that a lot of rules and norms were religious, and as such not real law. This claim was ethnocentric because it assumed only secular law is law. It was also hypocritical, because many Western laws — such as bans on abortion, adultery and homosexuality — are nothing but Christian norms dressed up as laws. But since India did not seem to have had anything resembling the system of royal courts that developed in Europe, it could more easily be said that Indians were rich in customs but lacking in (Western) law. In the case of China, however, which had a complex legal system complete with judges and an examination-based bureaucracy, long after the legal system of the Roman Empire had been lost and European barbarians were busy pillaging each other's villages, the law versus custom opposition could only be maintained through sheer Eurocentric fervor.

China had laws — written laws, at that, and laws administered by professional judges who issued written judgments. Chinese law was nevertheless not considered seriously by any but a few academic scholars. The people of China were said to be languishing under the arbitrary rule of "oriental despots" who did not follow the rule of law but rather issued decrees. (This belief is by no means dead today. The Walt Disney children's films *Aladdin* and *Mulan* reproduce the myth of "oriental despots" ruling through a combination of tradition and arbitrary decree, even if some of the despots happen to be benevolent.) The many innovations in state administration, including law, of the peoples of China were reduced to custom —

with custom having a rather negative connotation, as in the oft-used phrase "prisoners of custom."

Tradition and custom might be culturally rich, it was readily admitted by European observers, but they were precisely what modern law had to fight against. And this is true not only in the eyes of nineteenth-century imperial authorities, but in the eyes of some of today's international human rights advocates. For much of the nineteenth and twentieth centuries, tradition and custom were seen as hindrances to the progress of the rule of law. But it is now acknowledged that most traditional cultural practices, whether religious or secular, are worth preserving. Few if any international non-governmental organizations (NGOs) would now try to persuade African people to eat American food, for example. But tradition and custom are nevertheless regarded as potentially threatening the march of modernity, and specifically, the rule of law.

If the peoples of China and India with their venerable literate traditions could be regarded as "backward" because they supposedly had many customs but no real laws, the aboriginal peoples of Africa, North America and Australia were even more summarily dismissed as lacking in law altogether. Since Moses and his Ten Commandments, the Judeo-Christian tradition, and later the Muslim tradition as well, take proper law to be written law, and take legally binding documents and decisions to be ones that have been written down and preserved. The cultural prejudices of the "religions of the book" were transferred directly to Europe's modern legal systems. Real religious law came in books, or at least on tablets. So too, real secular law exists only in formally written texts.

Peoples who did not feel the need to develop formal systems of writing were thus considered to have no real law. The memorization of a clan's or a people's accounts of the relation between people, spiritual beings and land — a task that leaders of aboriginal communities undertake with great seriousness and care to this day — has never been regarded, by whites, as having anything in common with going to law school. Learning the narratives that set out what is right and wrong, what is to be done by whom and how, what duties we owe to the earth and to other human beings — this difficult and important task, which all cultures need to perform, was valued by Europeans only when carried out in formal institutions using books.

In Australia, New Zealand and Canada it is only in the last ten or fifteen years that regular (i.e., white) courts have begun to acknowledge that there is such thing as aboriginal law, even if it was never written down and even if it is not administered by professional judges. But the scope of aboriginal law is still extremely restricted. For example, an aboriginal offender will be convicted by a regular court using "normal" (white) law, and aboriginal elders will be involved only later in determining the precise sentence. No regular court in nation states dominated by the descendants of white settlers is likely to admit that aboriginal law is more than a quasi-legal or infra-legal kind of custom operating within certain exceptional spaces (reservations and other aboriginal communities). That aboriginal law might indeed be worthy of being treated as "the law of the land" on a par with white law — and thus potentially applying to non-aboriginals as well as to aboriginals, and to everyday transactions in addition to such restricted areas as hunting and fishing rights — is not something that can be contemplated by the existing legal institutions.

Law and Justice

Aboriginal legal thought is not interested in generating a great deal of law in the sense of particular black-and-white rules that have to be applied in the future regardless of whether they still have the weight of social norms behind them. Aboriginal legal scholars are not primarily interested in working out little rules about which clan can legally hunt over what territory at what time of the year. Rather they are concerned to clarify the general principles that underlie all specific rules and that remain constant as rules and norms change due to new needs or new events. Precisely because aboriginal law is not written down in treatises that are separate from the everyday management of disagreements and conflicts, and also because there is no body of professional judges separate from the body that passes laws, there is not much difference, from the aboriginal perspective, between law and justice.

In Western systems of law, by contrast, law is always separate from justice. Sometimes law seems to serve the needs of justice, as when we say that a particularly nasty criminal has been "brought to justice," meaning brought before the legal authorities. But the legal system has many other concerns besides justice. Vast numbers of minor offenders end up in prison because they cannot pay fines or because they missed a court date, not for the actions that led them to be in trouble with the law in the first place. This situation threatens the integrity of the legal system. Criminologists have long argued that justice is not served when large numbers of petty offenders — who are arrested for shoplifting or for having a few joints — end up serving longer prison terms than white-collar criminals who have pocketed large sums of money, or husbands who have abused their wives.

The fact that any breach of minor bail conditions, such as abstaining from all alcoholic drinks, is treated as a major criminal offense in white Western legal systems shows that the legal system's own authority matters more than reaching a just solution. This is also the case with the major criminal offense known as "contempt of court," which as far as I know has no equivalent in aboriginal systems. For example, journalists are sometimes charged with contempt of court and put in prison if they refuse to reveal a source when a court demands that they do. Similarly, in some North American jurisdictions, women who refuse to testify against their male abusers have sometimes been charged with contempt, an offense that can carry heavier penalties than those that might apply to the abuser. People such as these journalists and these abused women are hardly criminals in the ordinary sense of the word.

Ever since the rise of formal, written state law, questions have arisen about how citizens can tell whether or not the legal system is actually just. In aboriginal societies, law and justice are more likely to converge, since there is less formality and less concern about procedure and rules. But once the process of lawmaking and administering law is formalized, law and justice can easily go their separate ways.

In some cases it is fairly obvious that law and justice have parted company. Nazi laws targeting all Jews for harsh treatment were clearly unjust by anybody's definition of justice (see Legal Injustice page 51). The interesting question regarding these laws is not whether they are just or unjust, since that is obvious. The real question is why the Nazi government felt obliged to go to the German parliament and have their policies put in the form of law instead of merely using force.

By 1938 the anti-Jewish laws had expanded to prohibit Jews from owning businesses. The German Jewish philosopher Hannah Arendt later stated that, given the fact that Germany had a constitution setting out a parliamentary democracy as the system of government, the Nazis, while sometimes encouraging violence against Jews and others, took the law seriously, at least until 1939. Other historians have suggested that many

Legal Injustice

After coming to power in 1933, the Nazi government initiated a number of increasingly harsh restrictions on the Jewish minority. The Nazis were careful to make sure they drew up laws and passed them in the parliament. First, Jews were thrown out of the professional civil service (which in Germany includes university teaching) and the legal professions. The 1935 "Nuremberg Laws" went even further. Here are two examples:

> **Law for the protection of German blood and German honor.** Marriages between Jews and subjects of German or kindred blood are forbidden... Extramarital intercourse is forbidden between Jews and subjects of German or kindred blood... Jews are not permitted to employ female citizens of German or kindred blood as domestic workers under the age of 45...

> **First decree to the Reich Citizenship law.** A Jew cannot be a Reich citizen. [The Reich, meaning the kingdom, was the Nazi term for the German state.] Jews are not entitled to the right to vote on political matters; he [the Jew] cannot hold public office... A Jew is anyone descended from at least three grandparents who are fully Jewish as regards race... Also deemed a Jew is a Jewish *Mischling* who is descended from two fully Jewish grandparents and... who belonged to the Jewish religious community... who was married to a Jew...

Germans had too much respect for legalism and too little concern for justice. Only the communist left seriously organized themselves against the Nazi misuse of law.

The flagrant Nazi misuse of the legislative system is unusual. Much more common are situations in which a certain portion of a society believes that the government of the day and its laws are legitimate, and that if laws are passed restricting human rights or treating certain groups differently, this is justified because the very survival of the society demands it. In the US, for example, in the context of the "war on terrorism" that began in September 2001, the administration of George W. Bush held that extreme restrictions on the legal rights of certain groups (non-citizens as a whole, and citizens and non-citizens suspected of terrorist activities) could be justified as in keeping with the rule of law, even though many of these restrictions were flagrant violations of basic constitutional rights.

Since the ancient Greeks philosophers who have concerned themselves with justice rather than with the details of legal systems agree that justice is by definition impossible to carry out. For one thing, doing justice to one person or one cultural group might well necessitate taking something away from someone else, or doing damage to some other interest. For example, in the United States there are occasional calls for the government to provide reparations to the descendants of slaves. But it is difficult to imagine any practical way in which the massive injustice that was slavery can be undone. Reparations may well be worth pursuing for symbolic and political reasons, but a legal system designed to provide a remedy if one gets hit by a car is not suited to dealing with large historical injustices.

In addition, people, even those from the same cultural group, do not always agree on what it is that justice demands. Environmentally oriented legal scholars and philosophers argue that governments need to take future generations into account when making decisions about everything from garbage disposal to taxes. Justice means thinking about the future of humankind and of the planet. Politicians in developing countries, by contrast, often say that increasing production and employment in their countries now, regardless of environmental cost, is what justice — in the sense of lessening international inequality — demands. Everyone agrees that justice involves treating people fairly and improving the condition of humankind rather than selfishly seeking individual gain. But what exactly does that mean in a particular situation? Justice, as Plato suggested several millennia ago, will always be a matter for discussion and dialogue.

Fighting Injustice

The recognition that obeying the law is not the same as doing justice is something that is clearer to people living under dictatorial regimes. These regimes often pass laws — rather than simply using force — to carry out their policies. A famous speech given by one of the most noted spokespeople for justice in the twentieth century, South Africa's Nelson Mandela, illustrates this very well. At the 1963-64 Rivonia Trial that resulted in him being imprisoned for twenty-seven years, Mandela not only denounced South African apartheid law as unjust but stated that organized violence against the state was fully justified. Some people have argued that Mandela's speech supports certain forms of terrorism. Mandela says,

In 1960 there was the shooting at Sharpeville, which resulted in the proclamation of a state of emergency and the declaration of the ANC as an unlawful organization. My colleagues and I, after careful consideration, decided that we would not obey this decree. The African people were not part of the Government and did not make the laws by which they were governed.[1]

He goes on to say,

Some of the things so far told to the Court are true and some are untrue. I do not, however, deny that I planned sabotage. I did not plan it in a spirit of recklessness, nor because I have any love of violence. I planned it as a result of a calm and sober assessment of the political situation that had arisen after many years of tyranny, exploitation, and oppression of my people by the Whites.... We believed that as a result of Government policy, violence by the African people had become inevitable.... Secondly, we felt that without violence there would be no way open to the African people to succeed in their struggle against the principle of white supremacy.

Mandela believed that only violence would serve the needs of justice in the particular situation of South Africa in the 1960s, and that there was little point in hoping that international pressure would suffice to change the South African legal system. Other noted leaders of twentieth-century social justice movements, notably Mahatma Gandhi and Martin Luther King, believed that violence is always wrong, arguing that using violence taints and corrupts those who use it, however noble the cause.

Given the profound disagreements about general philosophical issues and about practical tactical questions concerning justice, it is safe to say that the relation between justice and law will always be under discussion and negotiation. And for many of the leading political thinkers, from the ancient Greeks to today, human beings are human precisely because we can and should think about our own situation, and talk with others about how we might listen to the demands of justice — how we might bring our laws a little closer to justice — without ever imagining that any of us have the complete solution.

Chapter 4
Who Are the Police?

In countries that are reasonably peaceful and stable, the question, who are the police? may seem to be a rather stupid one. Doesn't everyone know who the police are? Even small children can identify police officers, after all.

But do we really know who the police are, even in the most stable of nations? What about plainclothes detectives? What about airport security officers? Are they police or not? What about the civil servants who inspect our tax returns and scrutinize companys' financial statements looking for fraud? And what about the uniformed men (and sometimes women) who drive around public housing projects in cars that look like police cars but are painted a slightly different color?

In theory (i.e., according to the letter of the law), the one thing that police officers can do and others cannot is to use some force to arrest those charged with crimes. Every other job done by police, from patrolling streets to directing traffic to helping homeowners and businesses improve their security to gathering evidence of crimes, is also done by others. Private security officers patrol streets and businesses; school crossing guards direct traffic; alarm companies educate citizens about theft and robbery; and a host of bodies (from private detectives to civil servants to forensic accountants) take part in the multifaceted work of detecting crime and identifying culprits. But only police can use force to detain someone — and they can do so only when there is sufficient evidence that a specific law has been broken.

That makes sense until one discovers that the myriad private security guards and other uniformed personnel engaged in security work (e.g., border police, airport security guards) are authorized to make "citizen's arrests." These arrests are meant to be temporary, to hold someone until the "real" police can attend and take charge. While in the Anglo-Saxon legal system citizen's arrests are meant to be exceptions to the rule, like all exceptions, there are many real-life situations in which the theoretical divide between police and citizens breaks down. The police called to a public housing development or to a shopping mall by a private security guard are unlikely to treat the person apprehended by a citizen's arrest as "innocent until proven guilty" (a right of citizens in many democratic countries that puts the burden of proof on the prosecution in a criminal trial). Having an ongoing comradely relationship with their fellow uniformed forces of order, the police are unlikely to dispute the guard's version of events. The teenage shoplifter or the young man who made fun of the security guard are in a sense guilty before the police even arrive.

The key legal safeguard to protect citizens against arbitrary police power is the requirement that police have "reasonable and probable" cause to believe that a specific crime has taken place (not just that moral or social norms have been breached). Studies of street patrol work show, however, that police often focus on disorder and disorderly people rather than on actual, legal crime (see Chapter 5). Teenagers hanging out at a mall at an unusual hour, for example, can be charged without having done anything (especially in US municipalities that have age-specific curfews). The vague categories of "loitering" and "vagrancy" no longer exist in the criminal codes of most democratic countries, but numerous other laws — drinking in public, for example — continue to empower police to exercise control over the rowdy and the unseemly even in the absence of any evidence of crime.

While many agencies, both public and private, overlap significantly with the work of the police, police officers do not necessarily focus their energies on enforcing the law in a legally approved manner. The confusing fact that many police do not wear uniforms, while many other people in quasi-police uniforms are not police, tells us something not only about clothing styles but about our legal system. The answer to the question, who are the police? is not as obvious as it first appeared.

Who Is the Law?

Modern legal systems are meant to prevent private citizens, either individually or in groups, from using violence or intimidation. Legal systems are meant to ensure that only authorized agents of the state can, in certain highly limited circumstances, exercise coercion and violence against citizens. The use of physical force by agents of the state is subject to elaborate rules, with accused and convicted persons having the right to a legal defense and other rights. According to the German sociologist Max Weber's famous definition, a state is defined by the fact that it has a "monopoly on the legitimate use of violence."[1] People can only be deprived of their freedom after a complicated process — police officers need to justify their use of force, and so on. The state's violence is distinguished from the violence used by gangsters by an elaborate system of justification and limitation.

Organized crime and individual "enforcers" such as pimps and extortioners often manage to run private "justice" systems, sometimes for a long time. But even in the poorest areas of South Chicago, or in Mafia-controlled parts of the US and Italy, there is little doubt about what is the law and who are the law. It may be that people do not trust law enforcement officials, and it may be that law is somewhat powerless to enforce order. But only in extreme situations do ordinary people begin to feel that the state's violence is just as illegitimate and arbitrary as that of organized criminal groups.

For many decades, Colombia has been a notorious example of a country in which the legal system laid out in law textbooks or in legislation bears very little relation to the real world. A variety of guerrilla groups have at times controlled large swaths of territory, especially in the countryside, and have acted as the forces of law and order with little interference from official state authorities. In recent years, paramilitary groups (or military groups of citizens) have also developed. It is rumored that the military and the police turn a blind eye to the often murderous activities of the paramilitaries, since in many situations the paramilitaries have used tactics to restrict the scope of guerrilla activity that even Colombia's police would balk at using. For the paramilitaries, a stake in Colombia's lucrative drug trade is often a key driving force, and some say this is the case for at least some elements within the guerrilla groups as well. Thus the complicated and shifting lines separating one type of armed group from another cannot be predicted from political and ideological positions.

A major factor in the Colombian situation is that the sharp, even violent left-right divisions that have traditionally marked Latin American politics have over the past decade or two become overshadowed by questions of crime. In Colombia, as in some of the Latin American countries in which military dictatorships have given way to democracies, democratization has seen rapidly rising rates of violence and crime.[2] In Colombia, Argentina, El Salvador and Guatemala, citizens no longer fear being abducted and tortured by the secret police, but bands of more or less organized criminals (in some cases working hand in hand with corrupt police) keep the population constantly fearful. In Buenos Aires, for instance, the federal police in charge of the downtown enjoy a reasonable reputation. But some officers of the "Bonaerense" — which polices the much larger districts surrounding the capital where about 6 million Argentinians live — were implicated in a wave of kidnappings for ransom that took place in 2002, a time of severe economic crisis.

The end of military dictatorships and associated guerrilla wars in Central and South America did not mean an end to violence and insecurity. And if both violent crime and economic crime (including kidnappings for ransom) plague the continent, Colombia's citizens are particularly vulnerable. Exploiting the constant fear that is the fate of citizens in the nation with the highest murder rate in the world, both guerrillas and paramilitaries often impose a rough order in the towns they control by summarily killing thieves, drug addicts and other unpopular groups (e.g., transvestites).

Colombia may seem like an odd place to begin to explore the question, who are the police? But citizens who daily evaluate information and rumors — people whose lives depend on being able to accurately assess who is a thug and who is not — know much more about law, order and policing than any criminology student living in a peaceful country.

Colombia is famous among those who study law, order and policing. The longstanding problems of police corruption, military interference with civilian security and weakness of democratic systems that Colombia shares with most Latin American countries are compounded by the hugely profitable traffic in cocaine and other drugs and the constant American intervention into Colombia's internal affairs under the rubric of "the war on drugs." In Colombia the problem is not just that the forces of law are somewhat weak. In Colombia it is actually impossible when one witnesses the use of force to tell whether what one is seeing constitutes law or its opposite.

Anthropologist Michael Taussig, a regular visitor to Colombia since the late 1960s, illustrates the hellish dilemmas experienced by the unfortunate citizens of the war-torn parts of the country in his book *Law in a Lawless Land*.[3] In 2001 Taussig witnessed a paramilitary takeover of a town he had known for decades.

Other accounts (mainly by sympathetic journalists and international human rights workers) of how guerilla groups and military and paramilitary forces fight over control of the drug trade make it seem that only sheer terror keeps the citizens from rebelling against the violent order imposed on them. Citizens are portrayed as completely victimized and terrorized. This seems plausible, given the methods used by those who claim to be the force of "law and order." But Taussig realized that many people in the town who were not unsympathetic to left-wing politics were not mere victims. They supported the invading paramilitaries, and at times even praised them for "cleansing" the towns and villages of "undesirables."

The main reason for the unexpected popular support for a band of violent and often sadistic thugs was that the local police had never tried to protect the townspeople against crime and violence. Taussig reports that the jail languished unused, and the man with the title of local police inspector worked as a general-purpose municipal official, looking after everything except crime. Given this vacuum, the invading paramilitaries were able to gain support by addressing the crime problem as defined by most of the citizens.

In the small town (near the city of Cali, the world's cocaine production hotspot) the groundwork had been laid carefully by the paramilitaries before their actual takeover. For example, death lists had started to appear on the walls of the town, anonymously. Those targeted for death were not left-wing activists, the kind of people one might have expected the paramilitaries to target. Instead, the death lists were made up mainly of young men with a local reputation for violent crime. One such poster read: "If the justice system does not clean out the town, we will do it ourselves." And the list of names below used local nicknames and descriptions, as if to underline the fact that paramilitaries were listening to local information about crime: "Alias Sanchez, assistant at the bus terminal; Ruben Mejia, brother of the black man Perica; Castorina, the Indian…" and so on.[4]

Some of those named left town immediately. A week later, the town was plastered with new notices, reading: "Instead of trying to defend the lives of their sons and daughters that appear on this list, their parents should be disciplining them so that they stop being delinquents. Or do they have the right to mug, knife, and even kill the good people of this town?"[5] Under that heading, a different death list was found – this one containing not the names of ordinary small criminals but of corrupt town officials and noted drug dealers. Having already tapped into the local fear of crime, the paramilitaries now drew on local resentments about municipal officials' corruption. And throughout this intimidation campaign, they remained invisible.

A public meeting was called to discuss the lists. The locals suspected that the police had put up the posters and lists. The police attended the meeting and loudly complained that they were following the rules, that they did not resort to extralegal violence, that they were the "thin blue line" standing between the town's citizens and complete chaos. But the police had never been trusted. They had avoided looking closely into criminal activities, perhaps so as not to get in trouble with various groups, from the guerrillas to the political parties.

Indeed, for a long time the police had acted not as protectors of the people but as if they were the ones whose safety was at risk. They lived and worked in a kind of bunker in the middle of the town and only ventured out occasionally. When doing their rounds, they always went in twos or threes, and almost always in a vehicle rather than on foot. The police feared the guerrillas, who at various points had made incursions into the town and even controlled it for some time. But they also mistrusted the local population. This meant that when they were (incorrectly) accused of plastering the town with death lists, their complaints went unheard.

In a village nearby, Taussig noticed that the police station was next to the hospital. Someone told him that the police hoped that guerrillas wouldn't attack them for fear of injuring the sick, and that if they did attack, they'd be discredited for jeopardizing the only health service in town. Asking around, Taussig found that half the village wanted the police there to protect them against thugs, but the other half thought that the police station only made the town more vulnerable. Either way, nobody wanted to live anywhere close to the police station. And the view that the police were using hospital patients as shields against guerrilla attacks clearly undermined police-community relations.

Back in Taussig's town, the population had been softened up, as much by the wild rumors that followed the death lists as by the death lists themselves. After the rumors and fears had circulated for months and even years, the population was in a state of high anxiety. This meant that once the paramilitaries actually marched into the town, the event was not as unusual or frightening as it might have been. And since the paramilitaries began their reign not by executing trade unionists or left-wing leaders but by murdering drug dealers and unpopular people, many expressed some support for their actions, even if they remained highly critical of extrajudicial, vigilante methods.

How did this situation come to be? In Colombia, from the 1950s onward, much of the countryside has occasionally been controlled by one of two left-wing guerrilla organizations. When guerrillas, in Colombia or elsewhere, take over a territory, they do not simply brandish their AK-47s. They usually institute a kind of justice system. In Colombia each shopkeeper had to pay a bribe or tax (known as a "vaccination") for protection. In turn, the guerrillas maintained order. They might kill those suspected of spying on them for the state or for the paramilitaries, but most people could go about their business unharmed.

There are good reasons why the towns under guerrilla control are often described as "a state within a state." One reason is that the guerrillas, when they have seized control of a locality, act more like a combination of police force and tax inspectorate than like thugs. Taussig's informants told him that in neighboring villages controlled by the guerrillas, adultery came under control, and the consumption of both alcohol and cocaine was tightly regulated. Some towns controlled by the guerrillas even issued formal codes of justice covering criminal offences, family matters, alcohol sales and local sources of potential trouble, such as the use of unfenced pastureland.

Unfortunately for the villagers, the guerrillas gradually began not only to tax drug traffickers but to engage in some drug selling themselves. Eventually this drew the attention of competing paramilitary groups. This was the context within which the paramilitaries that Taussig saw in 2001 made their incursions into a number of towns.

When Taussig made a second visit to the town, in 2002, seventeen months after the arrival of the paramilitaries, he found that the paramilitaries were killing two or three "delinquents" a week (in a town of 50,000). Some of the victims had numerous friends, but even then their deaths did not result in an uprising against the paramilitary law and order. According to Taussig, "at most, people just whisper to one another at the funerals for the victims."

Despite the openly acknowledged lawlessness, Taussig notes that in 2002, after the paramilitaries had established their dominance over the town, the place did not look or feel like a war zone. Vandalism had disappeared, there was no breaking of windows or smashing of signs, the kids who made a living pushing carts to and from the market no longer fought among themselves, and there were no disputes in the streets. The paramilitaries had subcontracted some of their security operations to local gang members. The central plaza was full of smart new yellow taxis with two-way radios.

One of Taussig's friends says, about the paramilitaries, "They are assassins. I could never trust an assassin." But Taussig notes that she now "sometimes leaves the front door open during the day, something I have never once seen in thirty years."[6]

In the Colombian countryside, then, questions that might seem rather simple in a stable democracy — who are the police? or who enforces law and order? — are not so simple. Citizens have to make their own decisions about which force of law and order is the lesser of two, or even three or four, evils. If they pick as their sources of law and order groups that outsiders might think are "assassins" — the Taliban in Afghanistan or the paramilitaries in Colombia — we who are fortunate enough never to have faced those dilemmas should respect their decisions, even as we work to help ensure that in the future they have better choices.

The Persistence of Localism

When we make instant judgments about how poorly citizens of other countries handle their dilemmas about law and order, we act out of a deep ignorance of the circumstances that have shaped security and insecurity in other parts of the world. We're also acting without any real knowledge of how urban safety was provided in the heart of "civilized" Europe in the long centuries before police forces existed.

For example, in the eighteenth century, London, the largest city in the Western world, lacked not only a police force but even what we would now consider the basics of a criminal justice system. People who were victims of crime had to personally prosecute the offenders — there was no public prosecution service. Outside of London, they also had to personally apprehend the offender, or get friends or neighbors to do so, since there were no police. (London had some night watchmen, known for their predilection for drinking, who sometimes pursued and apprehended robbers and other criminals, but only at night.) And those accused of crimes did not have the right to hire a lawyer to defend them until the very end of the 1700s, so that even if an accused person had money (and of course most of them did not), no professional defense was possible. The absence of professional prosecutors and professional defense lawyers resulted in what is known as "trial by altercation."

One of the first modern police forces was Sir Robert Peel's London Metropolitan Police, founded in 1829, and its members were known initially as "Peelers" and then as "bobbies." Their distinctive helmets and expensive uniforms with shiny buttons, whose symbolism was borrowed from the military, distinguished them from the rag-tag body of watchmen and constables that had patrolled some districts of London during the night in earlier decades.

Reflecting on the relative newness of professional police forces is important because the English "bobby" — the friendly local constable who supposedly exercises a watchful eye over the community, tells tourists the time and helps little old ladies cross the street — has had a great deal of cultural influence in other parts of the world. An important factor in the worldwide spread of images of the trusted local bobby — and in the regular use of English police to train and help police forces in other countries — is that unlike nearly all other police forces, the English bobby does not normally carry a gun. The bobby's image is thus able to represent order without coercion, law without force — or at least without direct lethal force, since the bobbies have always carried heavy truncheons and, like other police forces, resort to riot squads and specialized military forces.

On the European continent, by contrast, where government control over political and cultural life was more common, police forces were closely modeled on the military, and were not clearly distinguished from the military for a long time. But in England, while parade drills, polished boots and other accoutrements of military life were borrowed in order to instill discipline, care had to be exercised in order to reassure the population that police forces would not interfere with "the rights of freeborn Englishmen." Local control was a key element in the strategy of legitimizing professional police. The same thing happened in the United States, where police forces emerged locally and remain to this day controlled by local politicians.

In the English-speaking world the politics of police forces remain to a large extent a local matter — something that goes against the grain of governance trends in complex societies. Despite the fact that many municipal forces, for example, the New York Police Department in the 1970s, have been known to be corrupt, with municipal politicians turning a blind eye to what criminologists politely call police "deviance," local forces have rarely been replaced by nationally organized ones.

This persistence of localism in police management is in keeping with the English-speaking world's longstanding suspicion of continental-style centralized control. Localism is also visible in such legal oddities as the persistent power of justices of the peace, who for centuries were simply local gentry or notables, and who to this day are generally middle- and upper-class quasi-volunteers with little legal training. In continental Europe, judicial work is simply a part of the civil service. But in the English-speaking world, and especially in England itself, criminal justice is much more locally rooted and controlled and much less professionalized and bureaucratized than elsewhere.

On the far reaches of the British Empire, however, there were no traditional local authorities (or none that white people would respect). Thus, the North–West Mounted Police (later the Royal Canadian Mounted Police) emerged in the late nineteenth century, partly to enforce criminal law, but largely as a military tool for suppressing aboriginal dissent and maintaining some control over the border with the United States. Today the RCMP acts as the local police in most of rural and Western Canada, a situation that shows that the dividing line between local forces and national police is not always sharply drawn. In Britain and in the US, national police forces only emerged late in the game and continue to exercise a limited jurisdiction, especially in dealing with national security issues, such as organized crime and terrorism.

In most of the English-speaking world, policing has been and remains largely local, which means that crime is generally seen from a local perspective. Despite the new visibility and rising prestige of specialized bodies such as antiterrorism squads, for citizens living under common-law systems the question, who are the police? tends to be answered by pointing to the local cop on the beat. The local cop continues to live and thrive in the collective imagination even though the realities of both crime and crime control make that highly local and largely uneducated figure increasingly irrelevant.

The Rise of Private Security

If the mythic power of the bobby prevents people from noticing the work of less visible and more specialized policing agencies, it also prevents people from thinking seriously about the rapidly rising numbers of people employed in the private security industry. Shopping mall guards, club bouncers, private detectives, bodyguards, gated-community staff, employees of global firms that rent out "peacekeepers" as well as mercenaries, alarm company workers — these and many other related occupations are providing a livelihood for more and more people and are changing the face of policing. It is estimated that in the US the ratio of private security personnel to public police is 2.6 to 1, with countries such as the United Kingdom, Canada and Australia having only somewhat lower ratios.[7]

In South Africa, a country in which private security has long been very heavily used, especially by middle-class whites, there are over 300,000 registered security guards (for a population of 44 million). There are also many unregistered guards hired not only to patrol private property but to provide bodyguard services for the middle classes, especially in crime-prone Johannesburg. South Africa's murder rate is the highest in the world. But while wealthier people are able to protect themselves and their property, poor and working-class people —

most of whom are black — are very vulnerable. They do not trust the national police, who they often associate with the brutal force of apartheid, and are usually left to their own devices.

The issue of who polices the private police is a difficult one. The public police do abuse their power, of course, but they operate according to publicly available protocols (or systems), and there are legal constraints on both the scope of their work and the means they use. In most places police forces are accountable to either municipal governments or state governments. Although a high degree of autonomy and even secrecy is often tolerated (even in otherwise "open" democratic societies), politicians must still exercise care to make sure that police force corruption and scandals are kept to a minimum. In addition, in most countries, news organizations assign specific reporters to dig up dirt on the police.

Private security firms, by contrast, operate with little or no accountability or transparency. They are legally private firms and do not have to open their books to the public. The legal status of their workers in relation to law enforcement has also been murky. In recent years many countries have moved to set up regulatory bodies to impose standards. In the UK a regulatory commission was set up under the 2001 Private Security Act. In the United States and Canada, federal governments have little or no power to regulate, but provinces and states have begun to set up minimum licensing requirements for both businesses and individual workers.

In South Africa, home to one of the world's biggest security markets, there is now a Private Security Industry Regulatory Authority. This body is concerned to raise the industry standards, particularly with a view to being able to provide professional — but private — security for the World Cup of soccer in 2010. It carries out inspections and sometimes initiates criminal proceedings against businesses or individual guards. But interestingly, most of its business consists of going after companies that don't pay their workers.

The underpayment issue highlights the fact that the private security industry — unlike public police forces — is sharply divided into two unequal sectors. At the top, if one can call it that, are specialized companies providing well-trained bodyguards and other highly paid experts who are hired, for example, to negotiate with kidnappers (in places such as Colombia or Somalia or Iraq) or engage in quasi-military work for private firms. Many of the employees of these firms are ex-members of state security forces, and are hired precisely because of their specialized knowledge. (For instance, the British general Michael Rose, who played a key role for NATO in the former Yugoslavia, now works as a consultant for a private security firm, which was unlikely to have hired him for his physical prowess as a bodyguard.) In many places senior police and military officers can make more money in the private sector, and private security firms prize their knowledge of military methods and their contacts in government.

But the majority of the 150,000 British and the 300,000 South African security workers are ill-paid, badly trained employees who spend days and more often nights doing dangerous work for minimum wage and few or no benefits. These workers are much cheaper than public police, and in many situations even municipalities and states employ private firms instead of public officers to ensure security.

To make the governance problems even more acute, sometimes private firms hire the public police for specific jobs. In North America this is known as "paid duty" work, which means police moonlighting for the private sector. Sometimes police forces work a kind of racket, in relation to private businesses, that has affinities with Mafia methods. For example, in Toronto, a city in which many large American companies shoot films and television series ostensibly set in US cities, the local police can demand that film companies hire a specified number of "paid duty officers" to do nothing more demanding than to guard the equipment. In this way police officers can pad their already generous paychecks, and police forces generally become more subservient to the private sector.

That the face of policing has been transformed by private capital is not just a matter of employment numbers, then, but also a question of who hires whom, who draws up the contracts, and who pays.

Chapter 5
What Do Police Do?

In theory, police officers are the only officials in modern societies based on the rule of law who are authorized to use force to detain and hold people. And this can only happen after legal criteria have been met. In democratic societies the key to such criterion is having reasonable grounds to believe that the people in question have committed a crime. But we have seen that in practice it is not always so easy to tell the cops from the robbers, the cops from the military, or the cops from the security guards.

It makes sense, then, that the related question, what do police do? is also more complicated than it appears. First of all, police are among other things workers, often working in large bureaucracies. Like many other workers, they spend a great deal of time avoiding work, taking breaks, shooting the breeze and, most importantly, filling out forms. All empirical studies of day-to-day police work show that "catching bad guys" takes up a small fraction of police forces' time. Even so, it would be misleading to assume that only the spectacular moments of law enforcement — such as the arrest of criminals — were real police work.

The other key finding of research on police forces is that when officers are talking to other officers, taking a coffee break or filling out forms, their lives are being shaped and changed in important ways. Researchers call the informal bonding that is fostered as officers hang out together at work and after work "police subculture." (Research shows that police officers socialize with other officers to an unusual extent.) Police subculture reinforces ideas about who is or is not a criminal or what is or is not a proper police problem. Police management staff and their civilian funders often engage in campaigns to change the attitudes of the police — for example, by providing anti-racism training or sensitivity training of various kinds — but these campaigns are often undermined and neutralized by the rank-and-file members.

In a police department in the province of Ontario, Canada, that had instituted sensitivity training in regard to gay and lesbian issues, for example, a rank-and-file officer showed up to work in a pink shirt. He explicitly told fellow officers that his pink shirt was a protest against the "gay training." This gave rise to sympathetic laughter all around. In this case, the biases of rank-and-file subculture prevailed over the efforts of well-meaning reformers: indeed, it is possible that the officers who participated in the anti-gay joking went out on their next patrol with increased prejudice against gay and lesbian citizens. And any officers who witnessed the incident who happened to be gay themselves would go away feeling a strong need to hide their identity. The pink shirt incident may seem trivial, but it is incidents of this kind that over time give meaning to the police officer identity — and make police subcultures unreceptive to attempts to make policing more democratic.

The effects of what police do in their working life can be grouped into four categories: keeping the government secure, catching "bad guys"/solving crimes, maintaining community order and exchanging information with other bureaucracies.

Keeping the Government Secure

The most visible police officers are those who patrol our streets and attend scenes of accidents and crimes. But virtually every country also has officers who are less visible, who in many cases never wear uniforms or otherwise call attention to themselves, who worry not about thefts and burglaries but about the security of the state itself. Some countries have had overt systems of political police, like the Gestapo in Nazi Germany or the KGB (a transliteration of the Russian initials for "Committee for State Security") in the former Soviet Union. But democratic countries also have political police. In Britain, for example, MI5 officers secretly collect evidence about potential threats to national security. Sometimes the state-security function is carried out not by a separate organization but by special squads within a national police force that also engages in crime fighting in the usual sense. For example, in Canada, the Royal Canadian Mounted Police can be found patrolling small towns in British Columbia and the prairie provinces, but there are also special RCMP squads devoted to organized crime or political threats to the government. And in other situations special squads within military organizations are given responsibility for identifying and interrogating potential enemies of the state.

These days, state-security policing is usually "networked policing" — made up of special units that include representatives from a variety of organizations. For example, many countries now have special squads that include immigration and police officials and that sometimes conduct joint raids on places of employment suspected of hiring illegal immigrants. Similarly, police forces from European countries collaborate in networks in which each police force (and each country) retains the power to make its own policing decisions, but in which information and sometimes resources are shared.

Government officials and senior police executives know full well that many of the most serious threats to government stability and state security are international in nature. The most sophisticated criminals are those who operate across national boundaries, for instance, selling weapons and drugs. But no effective system of international police has developed.

Interpol is often thought to be a special international police body, but in fact it is little more than an information-sharing network used by national police forces to

The Changing Focus of the FBI

On June 29, 1908, US Attorney General Charles J. Bonaparte (no relation to Napoleon) created an unnamed investigative bureau of thirty-four special agents within the US Justice Department. Congress was leery about this, fearing that the government was creating a secret political police that would work to further its political agenda. Congress therefore refused to give this force the power to carry weapons and make arrests. Agents had to ask for assistance from local police if they wanted to make an arrest.

At the beginning this tiny force investigated economic matters outside the purview of regular police, such as violations of federal antitrust laws and bankruptcy law. However, the moral fervor about women of ill repute that led to the passing of the federal Mann Act of 1910 gave the federal force new impetus. Now they could arrest men for "transporting women across state lines for immoral purposes." In enforcing this law agents began to target not only organized crime rings but also ordinary citizens who happened to be having love affairs. Left-wing citizens especially were targeted, because after the Russian Revolution of 1917 a "red scare" – a panic about internal communist threats – swept the US. The special and still unnamed agents were given responsibility for detecting "enemy aliens" as the US went to war with Germany and Austria-Hungary in 1917.

The name "Federal Bureau of Investigation" only began to be used in 1935, under its enterprising new leader J. Edgar Hoover. A wily promoter, he

pursue their own national priorities. Interpol has a small secretariat in Lyons, France, and seven regional bureaus spread out over a number of countries in the Global South, from El Salvador to Thailand. But its main "product" is a secure computer communications network that is used by national police forces rather than by any kind of international police force. The 2008 budget for Interpol was only 47.6 million euros — less than that of

successfully used both the media and the entertainment industry to popular-
ize his agency and push Congress to provide increased financial support. In
the 1950s and 1960s, the weekly television show *The FBI Story* persuaded
millions of Americans that, in the face of communism, a national security-
oriented police force was indeed necessary. It was only the extreme fears
associated with communism that succeeded in persuading Americans to
depart from the longstanding tradition of local sheriffs and municipally controlled police forces.

The FBI went through a crisis when the Soviet Union fell apart in 1989-
1991, because it seemed as if it would lose its raison d'être and therefore
its funding. However, relying on favorable news coverage and glamorous
portrayals in the entertainment industry (especially in the Oscar-winning
film *Silence of the Lambs*), the FBI was able to reinvent itself by claiming
special expertise in a supposedly unique form of crime — serial murder.
Legally there is no such thing as serial murder, and many psychologists
would also say that it does not make sense to think about people who kill
several victims as a distinct category. But by creating a special Behavioral
Sciences Unit and publicizing (in part through Hollywood films and television dramas) the idea that serial murderers are somehow different from
other murderers, the FBI encouraged local police forces to call on their
expertise. This is one example of how a police force can actively create a
demand for its services.[1]

many single-city police forces. Perhaps more important
is the fact that there is virtually no international criminal law that could be enforced even if Interpol were to
increase its budget. National police forces, while happy
to collaborate if they want a neighboring country to cap-
ture a fugitive for them, will never surrender their special
powers to enforce state-specific laws.

Even in the age of global threats, security forces and

other state-based bureaucracies operate almost completely independently from one another. The United States is interesting in this regard, since even within that country, the two main security-oriented agencies, the FBI and the CIA, have been notoriously reluctant to share information, much less coordinate their activities. The Commission of Inquiry into the September 11, 2001, terrorist attacks showed that institutional rivalries led to agencies not sharing information that might have helped to prevent the attacks in the US.

In the US the specters of communism and totalitarianism made American lawmakers overcome their traditional reluctance to have "big government" collect information on individuals, exercise direct surveillance of political activities and authorize funding for what became the FBI. Once formed, like all other bureaucracies, the agency put as much effort into preserving its budget as into fighting subversion — with serial murder and more recently "the war on terror" serving to give it new leases on life.

In the Soviet Union state funding was not subject to democratic parliamentary debate, so the KGB never had to discover or invent new enemies of the state in order to protect its budget. It did, however, have to keep abreast of every twist and turn of the Communist Party's shifting priorities, a particularly difficult task during the many decades in which the quite paranoid Joseph Stalin was supreme leader and virtual dictator. Formed in 1917 (under the name of Cheka), the organization that came to be called the KGB was more unstable than outsiders realized. For example, Stalin ensured that the KGB devoted a great deal of time and energy to tracking down Leon Trotsky, an important leader of the 1917 revolution. Trotsky was finally killed in the home of Mexican left-wing artists Diego Rivera and Frida Kahlo by Soviet agent Ramón Mercader, who stuck a mountain climber's ice pick into his skull.

For about eighty years, the KGB exercised close surveillance over millions of Soviet citizens, watching for potential threats to the security of the state — even if for most of the Soviet Union's history this security seemed to be synonymous with Joseph Stalin's whims. It also engaged in large-scale espionage using its own agents (often thinly disguised as diplomats in Soviet embassies) and by recruiting informers of other nationalities. In the 1950s the Soviet revolution still had support from many people in the West (at least until the Soviet suppression of the Hungarian pro-democracy revolt of 1956), so spies were recruited by appealing to the left-wing ideals of Western scientists and intellectuals. However, as the Soviet Union lost credibility among left-wingers in other countries, the KGB's espionage work came to rely mainly on people who sold secrets for purely monetary reasons, people who were thus unreliable.

In 1995 Russian president Boris Yeltsin signed the decree that disbanded the KGB, but he simultaneously created a new security agency that in recent years has been accused of many illegal tricks to suppress opposition to the Russian government of the day. And it is interesting to note that former president Vladimir Putin — who has clung to power despite term limits on the presidency by becoming prime minister — originally rose to prominence within the KGB apparatus.

The Russian government no longer tries to control the innermost thoughts of every citizen, but journalists who dig too deep into scandals risk being murdered. Dissent continues to be stifled. In contrast to the days of the KGB, high government officials now often use paid agents from Russia's burgeoning private security industry. But precisely because they are not government officials, these people can engage in "dirty tricks" without much supervision or fear of consequences. The November 2006 radiation poisoning and subsequent death, in London, of one of Vladimir Putin's most vocal opponents, Alexander Litvinenko, is a case in point. In the meantime, rates of violent crime in Russia have skyrocketed since the fall of the Soviet Union. As in many other places, it seems that the wrong people are being policed.

Catching Bad Guys and Solving Crimes

Preventing crime from happening in the first place is now often seen as the responsibility of a combination of local activism, neighborhood goodwill and vigilance, and paid private security. A bank worried about a spate of bank robberies may well contact the local police, but they will rely mainly on increased surveillance through privately operated closed-circuit television and on private security guards. However, once a crime has been committed, private security drops out of the picture. The task of finding out "who done it" and bringing them to justice is generally the sole responsibility of the formal, public police.

Television shows around the world give the impression that uniformed police and plainclothes detectives lead glamorous lives of crime detecting, featuring spectacular car chases and intriguing forensic evidence tests. The reality is much less thrilling. It is true that the work of locating criminals and ensuring they appear before a judge is the monopoly of the public police. But the success of this work is much more dependent on information from victims, neighbors and others than on any Sherlock Holmes-style brilliance. And in any case, the work of solving crimes and bringing "bad guys" to justice occupies a very small part of the public police's time.

Consider this: A New York City study conducted in the 1980s, a decade in which serious crime, especially murder, was at an all-time high, found that of 156 patrol officers studied, 40 percent did not make a single felony arrest in a year. (A felony is a serious crime, as opposed to the less serious misdemeanor.) Only 30 percent of officers made more than three felony arrests in a year.

But no matter how little time is devoted by each particular police force to catching bad guys, this is the only thing that distinguishes them from private security at one end of the spectrum and from the military at the other end. The unique legal powers of police forces — their ability to make arrests and initiate prosecutions — mean that it is crucial for all democratic societies to ensure that the police are indeed fighting crime in an even-handed manner.

Even in the most transparent and democratic societies, it is not easy to ensure that police are prioritizing the crimes that pose the most risk to the public, rather than arresting the marginal and the friendless while ignoring the crimes of the powerful. Police corruption is all too common. But even in forces that do not have systematic corruption problems, research shows that crime fighting is often marred by prejudiced ideas about who is or is not likely to commit crimes. In part because of the bias of news and entertainment representations of criminality, certain people "look more suspicious" than others, and factors such as race (as well as class, gender and age) tend to result in increased levels of suspicion.

Dozens of studies in the UK, in the US and in urban Canada show that black men are more likely to be stopped by police when walking and when driving, and are also more likely to be arrested if stopped than men of other races. This problem is known as "racial profiling." It is not the same as individual prejudice. An officer might not hold overtly racist views, and may well be friendly to fellow officers who are black, but still engage in stopping and searching disproportionate numbers of black people. Racial profiling describes an aggregate, systemic phenomenon — the correlation between race and negative attention by police or other authorities.

It is not always possible to determine whether a specific event is an instance of racial profiling. For example, in July 2009, renowned Harvard professor of black studies Henry Louis Gates was arrested outside his own home and charged with disorderly conduct by a white policeman. President Obama, who knows Gates personally, attributed the incident to police racism. This prompted a spirited defense of the force's fairness by the Cambridge police, which in turn led President Obama to cut short the dispute by inviting both the officer and Professor Gates to talk over a beer at the White House.

The incident is a good illustration of the difficulties that arise when one takes a term that was developed to describe a statistical phenomenon and tries to explain an individual incident with it. The facts are that on returning home from a trip to China, Professor Gates found he had misplaced his key and proceeded to break into his own house. A neighbor called the police. It is possible and perhaps probable that the neighbor thought it unlikely that a black man owned a house in the neighborhood. But it is possible that a break-in by a white male would also have triggered a call to the police, so it is hard to say whether the neighbor was acting out of racism. Similarly, whether the police officer was acting out of prejudice or not is difficult to determine. It was reported that Professor Gates became verbally abusive when the police arrived. His anger may well have come from his years of experience as an African American male living in a racist society, but there is no doubt that he was less than calm and collected. Even if we knew more about the police officer's private views, it would be unclear whether or not he would have arrested a white man in a similar situation. Thus, we cannot know for certain that the Professor Gates incident was an example of racial profiling.

While it is important to continue doing research to document the prevalence of racial profiling, we have to remember that profiling may continue to exist in situations where overt racism has largely disappeared, and blaming individuals is not the solution. A thorough change in the culture that surrounds us would be needed to really get rid of racial profiling. Having an African American male in the White House probably helps to change the general culture, but Professor Gates's own work suggests that a few individual stories (including his own success at Harvard) will not alter the fundamentals of American culture. And it is those fundamental building blocks of the culture that produce racial profiling.

Much work remains to be done to ensure that the core function of police forces, which is making arrests of people who have broken the law, is performed fairly and without singling out already disadvantaged groups. To address the question of the accountability of police forces to the public, most democratic countries have developed civilian complaints commissions and civilian oversight mechanisms, which are meant to ensure that crime fighting works for democracy rather than against it. These mechanisms are notoriously weak, however. In many instances the police merely investigate themselves, and in other cases officers from a different police force investigate their fellow officers. Rarely do civilians or even politicians have full access to the police's original data. Few if any police forces can justly claim that crime-fighting priorities and methods are transparently chosen in close consultation with citizens and their democratic representatives.

Maintaining Order

Criminologists have studied how the police go about their daily work by doing "ride-alongs" and closely observing how patrol officers spend their time. On the whole, these studies emphasize that patrol officers rarely encounter crimes in progress. And even when a dispatcher calls a patrol officer on the radio to report an incident at a specific address, much of the time there is no clear evidence of a crime. Many people call the police if there is a loud party next door, for example. And in many cities, local business associations insist that uniformed police be deployed in shopping areas to simply walk around and be seen — a use of resources that criminological research shows is not very efficient. The work that police do when attending calls about loud parties or walking around to satisfy the wishes of local businesses is not crime-fighting work. It is the work of maintaining order.

Research has shown that ordinary uniformed officers spend much of their time maintaining order rather than fighting crime. Numerous calls made for police assistance end up revealing drunk and loud but not criminal behavior. In these cases, which are common both in residential settings and in commercial establishments such as bars and clubs, the police often try to calm things down, separate people to prevent fights, and generally signal, by their presence, that things have gone too far and that order needs to be restored. In their routine patrol work too, police often stop people who are known to them or who simply look as if they are "loitering" — young working-class people, usually.

When police are asking young people what they are doing out late at night, or when they are intervening to prevent drunks from fighting, or when they walk around a shopping center ensuring that the alarm systems are functioning properly, they are not fighting crime, since no arrests are being made or planned. But the work of maintaining order in urban settings, both residential and commercial, is extremely important whether or not it leads to criminal charges.

In Britain, the Crime and Disorder Act was the legal flagship of Tony Blair's New Labour government, elected in 1997. The focus of the act was urban disorder rather than crime. One of the new measures contained in the act, and refined in subsequent amendments and related newer provisions, empowers not only police forces but a whole range of other authorities, including public housing authorities, to issue an "Anti-Social Behavior Order," or ASBO. Someone who persistently disturbs or annoys their neighbor or who regularly engages in disorderly conduct in public can now be issued with an ASBO, which is not a criminal proceeding, but which can lead to criminal prosecution if the conditions are breached.

The Crime and Disorder Act and similar measures taken in other jurisdictions to address disturbances that do not amount to crimes tend to assume that there is only one view of what counts as "disorder." These measures are always passed at the behest of businesses and those who represent "respectable" families. Young people, singles who like to "party," panhandlers, sex workers and cultural minorities are generally left out of the debate — they are somehow not included among "the residents" or "the community."

In the United Kingdom, where public order policing has mainly focused on young people hanging out in downtown public spaces, a clever new technology allows both private security and police to target youth — not middle-aged consumers patronizing restaurants and movie theaters. The "Mosquito" is a gadget that emits a high-frequency, extremely bothersome noise that can only be heard by people under the age of twenty-five or so for physiological reasons. (It's similar to the dog whistles that cannot be heard by humans.) The Mosquito is being used in many cities to disperse young people without even needing to talk to them or explain why they're being dispersed, as Leeds University criminologist Adam Crawford has documented.[2]

Police officers and many local politicians in Britain often deplore what is called "antisocial behavior" — as if contemporary cities are characterized by a homogeneous culture with a single moral standard. The fact is, some urban residents do not object to some noise and drunkenness and even some discreet drug selling. Indeed, the very businesses that are the subject of much police attention, especially during weekend evenings, go out of their way to create attractions — from crowded dance floors to loud music to cut-rate drinks — that cater to people's desire for excitement. This is in direct contradiction to police and politicians' talk about sobriety and order and civic respect. Some residents, on the other hand, may be early risers and nondrinkers, and may feel threatened by anything loud or unusual, by beggars, or by the presence of people who look as if they don't belong.

It is not possible to provide police officers with a specific checklist of what is or is not acceptable, given the sharp differences in lifestyle and values that characterize large cosmopolitan centers and even small towns. But the absence of a specific definition of order has not kept residents and businesspeople from expecting police to help keep cities orderly, or to at least keep disorder out of their sight.

The "Broken Windows" Theory of Urban Decline

Psychologist James Q. Wilson and police researcher George Kelling co-authored an article in *Atlantic Monthly* in 1982 that became the most famous criminological text of the late twentieth century. "Fixing Broken Windows" argued that the police should crack down not just on illicit activities but on anything that contributed to disorder and unsightliness. The authors developed the idea this way:

> A piece of property is abandoned, weeds grow up, a window is smashed. Adults stop scolding rowdy children; the children, emboldened, become more rowdy. Families move out, unattached adults move in.... Litter accumulates. People start drinking in front of the grocery...[3]

Wilson and Kelling were writing at the height of the American urban crack epidemic, at a time when both murder rates and inner-city devastation were high. In the early 1980s, before waves of gentrification had brought some middle-class whites back into the heart of American cities, parts of urban America were crying out for "fixing." Large areas of the downtown in cities such as Baltimore and Detroit consisted of abandoned properties and empty lots. At the same time, right-wing attacks on welfare payments and the flight of blue-collar jobs out of the US had reduced the ability of inner-city families to support themselves and to take an interest in maintaining the physical infrastructure of their communities. These inner-city communities, which in most US cities are overwhelmingly black, were the victims of social and economic processes beyond their control. But in Wilson and Kelling's simplistic view — later adopted by countless police chiefs and municipal politicians — they were to be blamed for their misfortunes. After all, why wouldn't someone fix a broken window? Why would someone stop picking up litter? Demoralized parenting and dysfunctional family life were real enough in inner cities of the US in the 1980s (and are still very real today), but in the "broken windows" discourse, the victims themselves were to blame for their economic and social misfortune.

The focus on minor infractions — for instance, jumping the subway turnstile to get a free ride — would later, in New York City, come to be known as "zero tolerance" policing. Zero tolerance was a clever slogan, because it was also being used by feminists campaigning against male violence and by highway traffic patrols intent on eliminating drunk driving. Given its popularity as a general slogan, it became difficult to argue that zero tolerance might be appropriate in regard to some behaviors, such as date rape, but not as a blanket approach to every kind of "disorder" one encounters on city sidewalks.

The Wilson/Kelling article did not talk about zero tolerance policing, but it paved the way for this approach, which was later embodied in British disorder legislation (beginning with the 1998 Crime and Disorder Act). It was then exported to other parts of Europe and even to Argentina, where in 2002 a major political party promised to implement *tolerancia cero* without clearly specifying just which behaviors were to be subject to this approach.

Since the article was written, crime rates have fallen in the US, the UK, Canada and most other developed countries. If police resources were allocated on the basis of documented need — as measured by crime rates — police budgets would have decreased over the last twenty-five years. Instead, the focus on "disorder" prompted by the article and its promoters has helped to keep police budgets up, as police have joined conservative politicians and fearful heads of family in campaigns decrying the disorder supposedly caused by homeless people, young people drinking in public or squeegee people, depending on the place.

The disorder campaigns are not merely plots by police to get more resources, however. They are also symptomatic of new fears arising from generational conflicts, global migrations and increasing inequality within cities. In continental Europe, for instance, Roma (gypsy) people emigrating from Romania and other Eastern European countries have been the target of fear-laden campaigns. Cities, especially city centers, have become highly contested spaces. Therefore, even though crime rates have been consistently falling, police powers and police resources have been increased in most places. The policing of disorder (as opposed to crime) is likely to remain a priority item for local governments and police funders for the foreseeable future.

Patrolling the Facts

Television dramas featuring police give the impression that the police lead fascinating and dangerous lives. Cops are shown successfully investigating serious crimes, chasing bad guys and (almost always) making arrests before the fifty-minute time limit of the show is up.

But in real life police officers only make arrests on rare occasions — once a week or so, for the average North American officer. The rate of solved crimes, even for homicides, is often low (below 50 percent). The truth is that the daily schedule of the average officer features a great deal of sitting around the station chatting with colleagues, recording information or responding to the requests of outside agencies for information.

Leading police scholar Richard Ericson, who spent decades following police around and seeing how they spend their time, concluded that police are no longer mainly involved in catching criminals (if they ever were). Police are now mainly "knowledge brokers."[4] What does this mean?

Officers spend more time recording who they have stopped or what places they have visited than anything else. And once they have recorded information, in the proper bureaucratic form, they then spend a great deal of time sharing parts of that information with other bureaucracies, a task that often requires reformatting or editing the information.

The content of the information that police officers generate, for use by their own employer or by outside agencies, depends on the political context. In a country such as China, where the police play a large role in controlling dissent, the police probably spend much of their time communicating with various echelons of the state and the Communist Party and sharing knowledge they have gained as they speak to citizens or patrol the streets. We do not know exactly what Chinese police do, since the Chinese government does not allow independent research on police to be carried out. But we know enough about the role of the police in Soviet-era Eastern Europe to make an informed guess that communications about political threats make up a very large part of everyday police work.

Apart from the surveillance work that all police carry out to some extent, but which those in undemocratic societies do more vigorously, police in all countries have to deal with routine traffic, road accidents, crowd control and security at cultural events and at tourist attractions, routine crime problems, and occasional emergencies such as floods or fires. All of these tasks generate huge amounts of paperwork. Political surveillance aside, police forces around the world generally carry out many information-heavy tasks, including

- routine criminal record checks for employment purposes
- reports on people such as immigrants and government employees in sensitive jobs
- stolen vehicle reports, traffic accident reports and information about break-ins and robberies for insurance companies
- providing routine security information to residents and to businesses, in person and in the form of pamphlets or videos
- reports of break-ins or suspicious activities

- communicating with courts and correctional
  institutions about people on probation or
  parole or about offenders.

Only the last two items on the list involve crime or criminals, and even they involve mostly paperwork.

Some readers might say that equating police to bureaucrats is not appropriate for most of the world. It is true
that in most of the Global South, a good number of
police forces are characterized by high levels of corruption.
The word "corruption" suggests occasional, under-the-
table wrongdoing for personal gain – that is, the opposite
of impersonal bureaucracy. However, corruption often
becomes so overt and so systematic—among police officers
as well as state officials—that the work facilitated by bribes
and other forms of corrupt behavior often resembles ordinary bureaucratic processes of information management.

A personal example may help to illustrate Ericson's
point that police are chiefly knowledge brokers, even
in situations of corruption. In 1990 I was visiting my
brother in Lima, Peru. My passport was stolen (a very
common occurrence at that time). I was not expecting
the police to actually apprehend the thief. But on visiting
the Canadian consulate to get a replacement, I was told
I needed an official piece of paper from the local police
certifying that my passport was stolen.

This request immediately implicated the Canadian
government in Peruvian police corruption, since everyone
working at the consulate must have known what my

brother quickly told me — namely, that the police would be happy to produce the piece of paper I needed if I slipped them some US dollars. My brother said to me, "I'm a local, so I'd probably get away with paying the cops ten dollars, but you're a visiting Canadian, so you'd better give them twenty." Clearly, there was a routinized price scale for police information.

I was fortunate that my brother had some US cash. (My money had been stolen along with my passport, and the banking system was then dysfunctional, which only added to the irony of the Canadian consulate demanding that I get a piece of paper from the local police.) So we marched to the closest police station. I explained my situation, handed over the twenty-dollar bill kindly provided by my brother, and got the required piece of paper with remarkable efficiency and politeness.

I then walked to the Canadian consulate with the piece of paper, where I lined up for hours. (I would have been happy to pay someone "under the table" to get service, but this option was not available.) When my turn finally came, I was told that to obtain a temporary passport to return to Canada, I would need a guarantor's signature. I therefore had to pay an extra fifty Canadian dollars to get the consul's signature. (The consul acted as a guarantor for tourists, even though of course he did not know anything about them, which rather defeats the idea of a guarantor.) The consul duly signed the guarantor form (after I had gone back to my brother for an additional fifty-dollar loan), and so I was able to get back to Canada.

The fifty Canadian dollars I paid to the consulate may not have landed in anyone's personal pocket. But given that the Canadian consul earned a very high salary, he had no incentive to pocket the payments. The Peruvian police, by contrast, needed to supplement their meager and uncertain salaries as state officials in many parts of the world do. Over time, the bad working conditions for state employees, combined with state structures with little investment in accountability, created a system of standard prices for official pieces of paper, a system that was not publicized anywhere but which everyone understood.

What linked the two agencies to one another (via the victims of passport theft) was the huge appetite for information that characterizes modern bureaucracies. My little misfortune illustrates the general point that whether done officially and legally or whether obtained by means of a twenty-dollar bill placed quietly on a desk, the production of information — not the pursuit of bad guys — is the key function performed by police in the contemporary world.

Police officers see what they call "paperwork" as meaningless, as something interfering with their real work. But the vast amount of time spent by police gathering information, recording it, re-recording it or inputting it, processing it, and passing it on to their bosses or to outside agencies is not in fact meaningless or useless. Police paperwork is a major contributor to the ongoing data explosion of our information age. Sometimes police paperwork is merely stored, but in many cases it is processed and re-formatted for future use. Police-generated data, which include facts about individuals as well as aggregate facts (such as the number of robberies in a particular area), are continuously disseminated to a variety of other agencies – not only to criminal justice agencies such as prosecutors, but also to insurance companies, the media, politicians and school boards.

Given the increasing importance of information management and information systems, it is likely that the information-brokering role of police forces will take an increasingly large share of police time — whether or not individual police officers become reconciled to the inevitability of what they always call, pejoratively, paperwork.

Chapter 6
Law's Harms

Health care researchers and practitioners pay a great deal of attention to conditions known as "iatrogenic" — an adjective that refers to attempts to treat or cure an illness or injury that end up resulting in new problems or harms. A scalpel left in someone's stomach by a careless surgeon or an infection acquired from hospital furniture are examples of iatrogenic conditions. There is no equivalent term in the field of law enforcement, but many observers have noted that laws and law enforcement policies often backfire and result in the creation of new harms. Prostitution and drugs are two areas in which enforcing the law often causes more harm than good.

Prostitution Laws

Although nobody believes that prostitution can be abolished through legislation, most countries put prostitutes on the wrong side of the law. Laws against prostitution expose sex-trade workers both to coercion and violence from pimps — whose hold over women derives in part from their ability to either bribe the police or watch out for them — and to other difficulties arising from being criminalized. Few jurisdictions imprison women simply for working as prostitutes. But in many countries, police officers harass and/or rape prostitutes with impunity. Being constantly liable to arrest further victimizes people who ended up in prostitution only because they were already marginalized and lacking in employment skills.

In the United States and in other English-speaking countries, the enforcement of prostitution laws has historically swung back and forth between two equally irrational strategies, that is, between encouraging prostitutes to congregate in brothels and red-light districts, on the one hand, and on the other hand, closing down indoor venues and thus inadvertently encouraging outdoor, individual prostitution.

In the early years of urbanization, in the nineteenth century, police would often allow brothels to operate discreetly in certain areas (red-light districts). Respectable people who did not wish to participate in or even see prostitution going on could easily avoid these areas. In many cases, the safety of prostitutes was enhanced by working in houses run by professionals, even though the employment conditions were usually very exploitative. However, civic reformers, especially in Britain and the US, regularly stoked the fire of public opinion and denounced chiefs of police for their informal agreements with brothel owners. Such campaigns led to police raids on red-light districts and the dispersal of prostitution around the city.

The sudden visibility of prostitution in turn provoked new complaints from residents, who were now exposed to the sights and sounds of sex-trade exchanges that had formerly taken place behind closed doors. Complaints from residents led police to turn a blind eye to indoor prostitution. This is the case now in much of North America, where escort services operate more or less with impunity, whereas women working on their own on the street are subject to police raids as well as to heightened levels of gender violence.

The century-old back-and-forth swing from red-light districts to the streets only shows the futility of criminal-izing prostitution. It also shows that concentrating on one type of sex trade (e.g., only brothels or only street workers) is myopic, since banning one brings about an increase in the other. But few politicians are willing to take a practical look at the problems experienced both by the women and by their neighbors and experiment with strategies to minimize the harm to everyone concerned. So-called toleration zones (streets or other small areas in which sex-trade laws are not enforced, by agreement between police, sex-trade workers and residents) have been tried in countries such as Holland and Germany, in some localities in England and Scotland and also in some Australian states. Sometimes these have proven successful in reducing complaints and increasing the safety of the women workers. But in countries in which prostitution remains criminal, such toleration zones are always precarious and unstable, since any police officer could decide to arrest either a prostitute or a client.

Local experiments with partial legalization are mainly driven by police frustration and by the demands of citizens. Citizens who live in inner cities usually recognize the failures of criminalization, but are rarely willing to involve sex workers in putting forward strategies to regulate the harms associated with sex-trade work. And when sex-trade workers are not happy with the arrangements that legalize some kinds of prostitution, the arrangements tend to fall apart (as has happened in some British cities).

The fact is that legalization has often resulted in highly oppressive working conditions (such as those prevailing in Nevada brothels or in the famous Paris brothels of the nineteenth century). In some counties of Nevada, prostitutes cannot shop or walk around the town whenever they want, and they are usually treated with great contempt. In addition, the brothel owners and managers usually keep most of the money.

These problems have misled some advocates for sex workers into thinking that legalization as such is harmful. But proposing that sex work become a completely unregulated type of work is not realistic, and would do nothing to ensure that the women who work in the business have pensions, health benefits and other employment benefits. Also, if prostitution were unregulated, it would be impossible to keep minors out of the business.

Some form of regulation is thus necessary. And as is the case with other jobs, every regulatory structure has its benefits and its drawbacks. But it is clear that the harms caused by using the heavy hand of the criminal law are great. Criminalization is particularly oppressive to the marginal women on the bottom rungs of the prostitution business.

When one considers the way in which the criminalization of sex work has exposed millions of women around the world to police violence, to exploitation by pimps, to unsafe working conditions (including violence from customers) and to the stigma of a criminal record, one can only conclude that criminal laws targeting sex work have been and continue to be a major contributor to women's oppression around the world.

Prostitution laws are by no means the only example of laws that create new harms. The US-led international campaign to stamp out illegal drugs is another example of how law-and-order campaigns can backfire.

Poppies and the Taliban

When troops from the US and other NATO countries invaded Afghanistan late in 2001, the hope was that the repressive Taliban regime would crumble, and that the troops and their civilian helpers would work toward reconstructing an economy devastated by decades of constant war. Almost ten years later, however, the troops are still engaged in military battles, and the basic infrastructure needed to revive an economy (e.g., electricity, transportation, schools) remains a dream.

In the absence of steady jobs in a normal economy, many Afghans turned to a traditional crop that is suited to the country's harsh and arid climate and that has an international market, namely, the opium poppy. The Taliban, during their short rule prior to 2001, had almost eliminated opium poppy growing. The Taliban's harsh puritanism opposed opiates for the same reasons that they opposed (and suppressed) alcohol and Western music. While during the 1990s Afghan opium poppy production oscillated between 50,000 and 90,000 hectares, in 2001 it fell to 7,600.

The new post-Taliban government, dominated by American influence, is not officially in favor of opium, but it has no more power to stop farmers from growing profitable crops than it has to stop roadside bombings. By 2003 the area of land producing opium poppies had climbed to 80,000 hectares, and as of 2005 it was well over 100,000.[1]

The American authorities in Afghanistan, noticing the increase in opium production, tried to resort to the same policies that they have used since the days of liquor prohibition in the 1910s — heavy law-and-order tactics — in this case, burning or poisoning poppy fields. That such tactics, especially in the absence of economic alternatives, would alienate the local population did not seem to be a concern. But a backlash against US policies is what predictably happened.

The Canadian network CTV reported in March 2007 that a large-scale survey conducted by a Belgium-based research organization polled 17,000 Afghans in sectors controlled by US and Canadian military forces and found that there was a marked shift in favor of the Taliban. Even those who were not sympathetic to the Taliban's fundamentalist interpretation of Islam told the pollsters that the foreign forces were harming rather than helping them, and in particular, that the new US policy to eradicate poppy growing was causing severe economic hardship. While still holding an official anti-opium policy, the Taliban, with its greater sensitivity to local problems, has supported the farmers, and has been able to capitalize on the US poppy-eradication campaign to increase their political support. Afghanis polled were invariably negative about the occupation, and 27 percent admitted (to Western pollsters) that they now supported the Taliban — a growth in support.

The Belgian report recommended that the US plan to eradicate poppy fields be replaced by a more sensible policy, such as trying to legalize much of the poppy crop by establishing an agency that would buy the crop and convert it into medical morphine. The British Medical Association also called to replace the poppy-eradication policy with a system allowing Afghans to become more economically self-sufficient through growing poppies to alleviate the global shortage of opiates for medical use.

In Afghanistan the US preference to ban the production and sale of "problem" substances merged with a misguided military policy to eradicate the Taliban by force. This law-and-order eradication strategy is similar to what was just discussed in the case of prostitution, which many American politicians think can be abolished by making it illegal. Neither opium poppies nor the Taliban, however, are likely to disappear, even if the US uses armed force, any more than men are going to stop using prostitutes if the sale of sex is made illegal. In fact, the heavy use of military force seems to be having the effect of making the population more hostile to the US-led occupation and more sympathetic to the Taliban. The current situation is thus a good example of iatrogenic-type effects. The remedy has turned out to be worse than the disease.

The Afghanistan situation illustrates a persistent feature of US international drug policy, which is the refusal to examine why Americans consume such a huge proportion of the world's supply of illicit drugs. Although in recent years certain countries (especially in Eastern Europe and in Asia) have seen rapid increases in drug use, the US remains the world's largest drug market. In Europe about 5 percent of the population uses drugs each year, but in the US the rate was 6.6 percent in the late 1990s and over 10 percent in 2003-2004. Using armed force to try to reduce supply does nothing except raise prices and/or move production around from one place to another, as long as the social and cultural factors that support the demand for drugs are left untouched.

Cocaine and the Militarization of Latin America

As communism was rapidly fading from the horizon in the late 1980s, US president Ronald Reagan declared illicit drugs to be the next big enemy. He said they constituted the most serious threat, not so much to the health of Americans, which would have been a valid argument, but to national security.[2] Domestic users began to be more heavily policed, as local police forces obtained new funding targeted at drug busting. The supply of drugs, particularly cocaine from Latin America, became the target of astonishingly expensive efforts.

President George W. Bush continued this "war on drugs" with the "Andean Initiative." The key policy plank was for the US to provide funding and new military hardware so that Latin American governments themselves could pursue coca growers and cocaine traffickers. That any policy working through local military establishments would be bound to cause more harm than good could have been predicted.

But the discourse about drugs as the great new post-communist threat was powerful enough to quash concerns about militarized strategies to suppress the drug trade. The US gave millions of dollars so that governments in Colombia, Bolivia and Peru could buy expensive weapons, helicopters and planes capable of eradicating crops by dumping toxic herbicides.

Scholars who have studied the effects of the Andean Initiative (and its successors) have concluded that local campaigns to eradicate crops have sometimes succeeded, but only to result in coca production springing up in another location, perhaps across a national border. UN estimates for Latin American coca bush cultivation tell

South American Coca Bush Cultivation in Hectares[3]				
Year	Bolivia	Colombia	Peru	Total
1993	47,200	39,700	108,800	195,700
1995	48,600	50,900	115,300	214,800
1997	45,800	79,400	68,800	194,000
1999	21,000	160,100	38,700	220,600
2001	19,900	144,800	46,200	210,900

the story of coca production being moved around rather than eliminated.

Reports since 2001 indicate that coca bush production has decreased to around 175,000 hectares. This may be more a result of the waning of the crack cocaine epidemic in American inner cities than any success at the point of supply. Eradication campaigns and brute military force may affect local production, but they do not change the basic fact that thousands of otherwise very poor Latin American farmers find it more profitable to grow coca — despite the risk of having the crops wiped out — than to engage in other economic activity. The cost of these largely unsuccessful efforts to stop Latin American farmers from growing coca is huge:

- The US sells more than $300 million worth of weapons and military equipment to Latin America every year.
- Between 1997 and 2002, the US spent over

$3 billion on military and police "aid" to Latin America and the Caribbean.

- About $1 billion in cocaine revenue flows every year to the Colombia-based guerrilla group FARC. Probably even larger amounts flow to right-wing paramilitaries that control much of the drug trade.

It is clear that the US's desire to export their war on drugs to Latin America has had the counterproductive result of creating new harms, including giving more power and resources to military forces that in many cases have a murky history of human rights abuses and undemocratic uses of power. Funding crop eradication and the policing of the narcotics trade also means that little money remains available for more helpful forms of aid.

In addition, countries in Latin America are eligible for aid — including health-related aid — only if they prove they are fighting the war on drugs in keeping with US policies. Because of their traditional dependence on the US, and their need to prove that their internal domestic policies and internal law enforcement are in keeping with American prohibitionist beliefs, Latin American countries have not been able to experiment with more enlightened policies borrowed from Europe. For example, needle exchange programs that reduce HIV transmission among injection drug users are vehemently opposed by the US government. While numerous such programs exist in Europe (and a few in Canada as well),

Latin American countries cannot try them for fear of losing their precious "certification" status.

The US-led international system of drug control has not only failed to suppress or even diminish the consumption of harmful drugs such as cocaine and heroin but has created new harms. Sovereign nation states, especially in Latin America, have been unable to implement innovations in policy that would be more in keeping with the economic and cultural facts on the ground. And given the American preference for law-and-order solutions, having drug policy dictated by the US has resulted, intentionally or not, in the strengthening of Latin American military apparatuses, with a consequent loss of resources for social services and health.

The War on Drugs in American Cities

US federal government spending on anti-drugs initiatives rose from $1 billion in 1981 to $17.1 billion in 1999.[4] During this same period drug consumption in the US increased by about 300 percent. The war on drugs did not even have the effect of raising prices. The effort to reduce supply only succeeded in displacing some sellers in favor of others. And the targeting of major organized drug networks had the effect of opening up opportunities for smaller entrepreneurs. So the price of drugs, on the whole, dropped, making them more accessible to young people and the unemployed.

The war on drugs did not succeed in eliminating drug use or making it more difficult, despite the huge amounts of money spent. But this does not mean that it had no effects. Inner-city communities, particularly African American communities, have in the past three decades undergone a series of highly negative changes. The effects of drugs policing are impossible to separate from the effects of other harsh right-wing policies (e.g., drastic cuts to social assistance, a severe fall in blue-collar jobs previously held by African Americans as well as whites, and law-and-order policies favoring long-term imprisonment, such as "three strikes and you're out" sentencing laws). But experts agree that the war on drugs has contributed to a huge increase in racial inequality. Now a vast underclass of racialized Americans are at high risk of going to prison or suffering the stigma of being on probation. Government policies often interact in negative ways. For instance, it used to be easier for African American women to get welfare for themselves and their children. A high rate of male imprisonment thus has worse effects on communities now than would have been the case before welfare law was changed.

While the intention of lawmakers might have been to target drug addiction and drug sales, the actual effect of harsh drug laws is to move very large numbers of people, mainly young men, out of the "reserve army of labor" and into the prison system. The negative effects of the war on drugs and the related constellation of policies on African American communities include the following:

- Between 1980 and 2000, the US prison population increased by 300 percent. From a prison population that was already high by international standards (half a million) the number of people in prison – excluding those awaiting trials in jails – went up to nearly 2 million.

- African Americans make up 13 percent of the American population, but in 1999 about 46 percent of sentenced prisoners (both federal and state) were black.[5]
- Among men born between 1965 and 1969, 20 percent of blacks but only 3 percent of whites had served time in prison by their early thirties.

Many activists and scholars in the US have been pondering the significance of what has come to be known as the "mass imprisonment" of racial minorities. Some point out that there's a curious correspondence between vanishing blue-collar jobs, fraying safety nets and mass imprisonment. The million and a half Americans who are currently in prison are not swelling the unemployment or welfare rolls. They are thus helping to keep official unemployment figures low. The larger context is that if you were a black or Hispanic male and dropped out of high school in 1955, you could get a factory job, which had a good chance of being unionized. If you drop out of high school today, selling drugs may be the only economic activity that provides you with a chance to get out of poverty and lifelong under-employment. Today there are few unionized blue-collar jobs available, and there are very few social assistance programs to support poor inner-city families. Mass imprisonment may have been designed to target drugs. But whatever the intentions of the legislators who passed the tough drug laws, the effect may be to disguise the absence of viable non-criminal alternatives to dire poverty in American inner cities.

As we saw in the first chapter, law can be a resource for communities seeking democratic reform and fairness. But many laws and justice policies, including those governing prostitution and illicit drugs, have created a range of new harms — in the Global North as well as the South, in the black neighborhoods of Chicago as well as in the mountains of Colombia. In addition, law-and-order policing strategies are often counterproductive, and when they succeed, they usually succeed only in transferring the problem from one place to another. A police raid on one sex worker's "stroll" will result in the business moving to another street, and the eradication of coca growing from one area of Latin America will result in the business moving to another region or country, as long as the economic and social conditions make both prostitution and coca growing a realistic option for many people.

Just as physicians must be careful that the medicines they prescribe don't cause more harm than the conditions being treated, so too politicians and the citizens to whom they are accountable should always be careful about the use of law.

Chapter 7
The Politics of Policing in Democratic Societies

Traditionally, police forces have been hierarchical and somewhat secretive organizations that are not run democratically and that have an uneasy relationship with their democratically elected political masters, such as city councils, legislatures and government ministers. The history of police organization and police reform is a long series of attempts to "police the police" to ensure that law enforcement priorities and policies are in agreement with the values and practices of democratic societies. These reform efforts have often gone under the banner of "civilian oversight."

The principle of civilian oversight is easily understood in regard to armed forces. Citizens of democracies, and indeed soldiers themselves, generally understand that decisions about sending soldiers to fight in a war or to engage in peacekeeping or disaster relief work are not decisions that should be made by military authorities. Heads of state or ministers of defense, who are usually elected and are part of an elected government, make the key decisions. Legislatures are usually involved as well.

The principle of civilian oversight is not as well understood in regard to police forces, however. There are civilian police services boards or boards of commissioners of police in the US, Canada and other jurisdictions. They usually consist of a mix of citizens and elected officials. They tend to exist only at the municipal level, however, with national-level police forces accountable only to a minister or top (civilian) government official — a situation that does not promote transparency.

Even when there are civilian police services boards, their role is limited. Usually the most important thing they do is to hire or (very rarely) fire the chief of police. They can also set policy in a general manner. But police chiefs have jealously guarded their quasi-military power to run "their" force, and only the chief can actually issue orders to subordinates.

For example, in Toronto in 1999 a progressive city councilor who was also a member of the Police Services Board was forced to resign from the board. During a demonstration that was threatening to erupt into violence, board member Olivia Chow had reportedly yelled at mounted police officers who were getting ready to charge the crowd. This was seen as interfering with the chief's monopoly on what the police call operational decisions. The distinction drawn by both police chiefs and politicians between "operational" decisions and more general policies is a curious one in the context.

In Toronto, city councilors often micromanage the operational priorities and indeed even the daily work of other (non-police) municipal employees. The officials to whom those employees report may complain or may end up ignoring what the city councilor has said, but they do not claim that they are autonomous and beyond criticism by elected officials. Municipal inspectors even joke about their "stop, drop and roll" policy, meaning that when they receive a phone call from a city councilor, they have to stop whatever it is they are doing and get in their vehicles to "roll" to the location generating the complaint. If anything of the sort took place within a police station, there would be a hue and cry about political interference.

Police forces have also perfected techniques to impede close scrutiny of their internal workings. For example, in Toronto police budgets go for approval to city council with a global figure for, say, "intelligence" without any breakdown. City councilors who inquire into the details will be told that the police cannot reveal secrets such as how many informers there are and how much they are paid. But without revealing names or the details of particular operations, police forces could provide a lot more information about how their money is being spent to the taxpayers who pay their wages. For example, I have tried over the years to obtain information on the costs of maintaining a mounted unit in Toronto (a city where the use of horses is limited, given the built-up environment and the amount of snow and ice). This information is simply not available to the public, or even to me, the director of an internationally renowned center of criminology located two blocks from Toronto police headquarters.

The details of police horse costs and other mysteries of police budgets may not seem related to the questions of democracy and the rule of law. But in modern government organizations, accountability — and hence democracy — functions through budget mechanisms. Governmental organizations, including police forces, have to draw up budgets and seek approval from politicians or other government officials or both, and they have to report in detail on how they spend the funds. Asking the people or the people's representatives for permission to spend money and giving an account of how it is being spent are the two crucial components of government accountability — indeed, they are the historic foundations of the rule of law.

Those concerned with democracy and justice thus need to learn to take a good look at how money is allocated and spent. In many Global South countries financial corruption is a huge problem within police forces, since bribes are often openly collected not only from those in trouble with the law but also from business owners, taxi drivers, hawkers and ordinary citizens. That kind of direct, more or less open corruption is clearly a huge impediment to democratization. But even in countries such as the UK, the US and Canada, where direct bribes to police play a small role, transparency and democratic accountability are elusive.

All bureaucracies, including police forces, have a tendency to prefer secrecy to openness, and to look after their own interests more closely than the interests of the clients or citizens they supposedly serve. In the case of police forces this systemic problem has usually been compounded by officials who cater to the "law and order" constituency — politicians and government officials who are afraid to stand up to police authorities, or are afraid to be seen standing up to police.

Civilian oversight is thus a principle that remains unimplemented or only partially implemented in virtually all jurisdictions. Recently, there have been many high-profile inquiries into police racism or other police wrongdoing — such as the Stephen Lawrence inquiry into the police shooting of a blameless black youth in the UK, resulting in an important 1999 report. These inquiries and reports are usually one-time deals, however. While they sometimes instigate much-needed reforms, they are not a substitute for ongoing democratic accountability and the kind of sustained, thoroughgoing civilian oversight that is the appropriate way to govern policing in a democratic society.

Another area that regularly receives attention from the media and citizens' groups, but usually only in a reactive manner, concerns citizen complaints processes. Until very recently, in virtually all of the English-speaking world, a citizen who wanted to complain about her or his treatment by a police officer had to go to the police station itself, report to a police officer or civilian police employee, and hope that the police force would investigate its own member. This is clearly inadequate and unfair, and in many jurisdictions citizens can now direct

Tasers

Police forces around the world increasingly use Tasers. The Taser is a stun gun that delivers a high-voltage electric shock that causes the target's muscles to contract. The target is immobilized and slumps to the ground. The Taser has been promoted as a non-lethal alternative to a gun, but it can be fatal, especially in the case of people under the influence of alcohol or drugs. This is important because it is against people who look disturbed or drugged that the weapon is most often used. Toronto police chief Bill Blair reported that in 2006 city cops used the device in 156 incidents, and in all but nine, the subject appeared to "have a mental disorder" or was "in some sort of crisis."[1] Reports from Australia and elsewhere confirm that people who look drunk, mentally ill or drugged are those who are most often "tasered." Moreover, an Amnesty International study of ninety-eight people who died after being tasered found that 90 percent of them "were unarmed and many did not appear to present a serious threat."[2]

Unlike hand guns, which are manufactured by a large variety of competing firms, Tasers are a branded product made exclusively by Taser International Inc. What is troubling is that police forces generally use the training and handling instructions issued by the very corporation that has a financial interest in selling more Tasers. And sales are high. Taser International says that its stun guns are being used in forty-four countries by more than 13,400 military, law enforcement and correctional agencies.[3]

In the United Kingdom only a few forces let ordinary police officers use Tasers, and then only as an alternative to shooting someone who appears to

their complaints about police abuse of power to special bodies.

However, merely having an arm's-length committee, not appointed by the police or composed of police officers, does not guarantee true independence. Throughout North America there are numerous independent police be seriously threatening police or citizens. In North America, however, Tasers are used widely. Civilian use of Tasers is prohibited in Canada, but not in the US, where they are available in most states. (The consumer Taser costs $299 and comes in pink — presumably for "ladies" — as well as in other colors.)

Between 2001 and 2008, 334 people in the US and 25 in Canada died after being struck by Tasers.[4] On October 14, 2007, Robert Dziekanski, a Polish man, died after being repeatedly shocked with a Taser by the RCMP at the Vancouver airport. He had come off a very long flight from Poland, spoke no English and appeared to be confused or disturbed. The subsequent inquiry revealed that the officers who responded to the call did not bother to consider less violent alternatives — such as obtaining the services of an interpreter — and proceeded to deliver not one but five electric shocks, despite the fact that, as video footage showed, the officers were never in any danger. The inquiry was widely publicized internationally. The recommendations made by former British Columbia judge Thomas Braidwood at the end of the inquiry in July 2009 included the need for province-wide standards and for officers to be satisfied "that no lesser force option or crisis intervention technique has been, or will be, effective" before using a Taser.[5] The Canadian Broadcasting Corporation reported in August 2009 that Taser International planned to challenge Braidwood's findings at the BC Supreme Court. Although the Dziekanski case and similar incidents have prompted some governments and some police forces to revise their Taser policies, it is clear that the growing use of Tasers will continue to be a concern for citizens in many countries.

complaints bodies. They can hear complaints and adjudicate them (that is, make a binding decision), but they almost always have to rely on police themselves to investigate, since they lack the authority to question officers and demand documents. Even in Britain, which on the whole has a better history of police-citizen relations than

most countries, it was only in 2004 that a fully independent police complaints body was set up, one that can do
its own investigation as well as adjudication.

One problem is that police forces are usually able to
stonewall outside investigators. Outsiders by definition
do not know how information is collected and kept or
what information is likely to exist or not. Investigators
who are not themselves current or former police officers
are unlikely to have the inside knowledge that would
ensure that they know what questions to ask or where
to look.

Much well-intentioned energy is being spent in a
number of countries on the question of independent
complaints bodies, but it is likely that no really successful system will develop until there are broader reforms
to ensure democratic accountability on an ongoing,
everyday basis, and not just in response to after-the-fact
complaints.

Community Policing

For about twenty years, police managers and government
officials in all parts of the world have been singing the
praises of "community policing." Its success is mainly
due to the fact that the term has no specific meaning.
Like "freedom," it can be used by any group to promote
any number of conflicting projects.

Community policing can sometimes mean that police
forces draw on communities for information and for help
with law enforcement. Adam Crawford's study of the

partnerships (involving police forces, citizens and businesses) mandated by the British Crime and Disorder Act of 1997 showed that in many cases the committees that were set up empowered the police much more than they empowered the community.[6] This was especially true when police influenced the choice of committee members. In many situations, the people (often black middle-aged women) supposedly representing "the community" explained the police point of view to the community rather than the other way around.

In addition, police often end up using their community contacts to gain information about illicit activities that they would not gain on their own. So a key question in examining community policing projects is, does the committee or other mechanism empower the community and make policing more accountable? Or does it empower the police to continue doing what they were doing all along but with more information and a new veneer of accountability?

If the first question is about whether the initiative empowers the police rather than the community, the second question is, who is considered to be part of the community? In general, police forces everywhere are much happier to have discussions with and listen to the concerns of business owners and middle-class heads of family than to understand the life situation of groups that are especially vulnerable, such as illegal immigrants, unemployed youth, homeless people and women sex-trade workers. When police forces are told by their own chiefs or by their political masters to go out and talk to the community, certain groups seem to be the "natural" representatives. And of course these groups — business owners and respectable middle-class families — are more vocal, more comfortable speaking to people in authority, and more organized than the vulnerable groups. In forming partnerships with community groups that only represent certain already privileged sectors, police forces may be worsening the existing relationships of domination and exclusion.

A third question arises when the work of law enforcement is transferred, either by conscious design or by accident, to community groups. If the community is dysfunctional, demoralized or seriously divided, can self-policing really work? Two studies, both on Kenya but one dealing with Nairobi and the other with rural areas, help to illustrate the perils of informal, bottom-up community policing efforts.

The crime concerns of Nairobi downtown merchants were addressed by working to obtain better resources for the local police, including a new Land Rover bought by the merchants' association and higher rates of pay for officers.[7] (Throughout the Global South, low police pay scales are associated with high levels of corruption, although corruption may exist for other reasons as well.) This police-business alliance achieved some improvement in street crime levels, but it empowered only business owners, not ordinary citizens. And the crime-control initiative did nothing to tackle the basic problems of corruption and arbitrariness that pervade both Nairobi City Council and the Kenyan national government.

Some communities in Kenya pursued a different strategy, replacing the discredited public police by neighborhood-based systems of volunteers or quasi-volunteers. The dangers inherent in such a situation are illustrated in a 2007 study of rural crime control in Kenya.[8] Cattle stealing is the major form of crime in certain areas, and in the 1990s community efforts to defend property sprang up in both Kenya and neighboring Tanzania — self-policing groups known as *sungusungu*. These groups set up an informal system not only to prevent cattle stealing but to pursue offenders and confine them in special cells. People were happy that their cattle were now safer, and the police eventually tolerated the new informal justice system. However, as often happens in such situations, the power to wield physical force changed the behavior of many of the men involved in pursuing and arresting suspected thieves. The men acting as informal sheriffs were often drunk and undisciplined, and sometimes killed the suspects instead of bringing them to the village for a justice process. And many internal disputes arose because there was no unified local community, but rather loosely associated families and lineages.

The idea of community policing assumes that there is a relatively cohesive community that has a certain set of safety and security needs. In situations where this is not the case due to the legacies of war, rivalry and sometimes even genocide, it does not make sense to borrow community policing strategies that may have worked elsewhere.

Since the fall of apartheid South Africa has witnessed a number of well-documented efforts to either supplement or completely supplant public police forces thought to be systemically corrupt, incompetent and/or arbitrary. Many community activists have worked to implement a variety of crime-control and peacekeeping strategies in shantytown communities, with varying degrees of success. One such initiative, undertaken by the Community Peace Foundation of Cape Town, is particularly innovative in that it recognizes that volunteers involved in protecting their communities and solving disputes among neighbors need to be recognized and, indeed, need to be paid — especially given that the NGO employees who are often the catalysts for such initiatives generally work for pay.[9]

When police forces are either absent or untrustworthy, bottom-up initiatives to improve citizen safety and security make sense, but these work best when the local community is already reasonably cohesive and motivated. When there is cohesion and trust — as happens in situations in which a whole people is rising up against a tyrannical government, for example — those who act as peacekeepers or security personnel are more likely to work fairly and accountably. Such communities are also likely to have trusted leaders who can ensure that arbitrary vigilantism does not develop. But when communities become dysfunctional and/or are divided by ethnicity, politics or lineage, giving some of the powers exercised by the public police to the community can create more problems than it solves, since the vulnerable may become even more vulnerable.

There is, therefore, no one recipe for democratic and accountable law enforcement. In some situations police forces, despite their tendency to secrecy and to pursue crime control without much concern for broader issues of justice, can and have been made more transparent and more accountable to the people, or at least to some representatives of the people. But in situations where much of the state apparatus is corrupt (such as in Kenya or Zimbabwe), it may be pointless to try to reform the police. Informal neighborhood or village systems for ensuring safety and security may be preferable to calling in the public police, but these too have their dangers. Groups in civil society can abuse power as much as police officers, after all.

A prominent policing scholar, Clifford Shearing, who was centrally involved in the attempt to reform the South African national police in the immediate post-apartheid period, came to the conclusion that the best solution to the dilemmas of law enforcement is to provide a budget for policing that each community or municipality can spend as it sees fit. If the public police have the confidence of the local citizens, then they will get the contract for police services. But if they don't, then the local government can hire private security or community groups to do the work, or experiment with combinations of different kinds of personnel for different purposes.[10]

This approach has certain virtues. If police forces had to compete with other security providers, there might be more stimulus for internal reform, and there would be no need to resort to the notoriously weak civilian oversight systems. But there are also disadvantages. Allowing the state to abdicate its responsibility for providing democratically accountable policing services to the population might end up rewarding the communities that have the resources to pressure governments and international NGOs for more and bigger grants, while further marginalizing the poorer ones. In addition, many of the disadvantaged communities who are often the target of police prejudice — homeless people, the Roma of Europe (gypsies), prostitutes, gays and lesbians — are not geographically concentrated. Being dispersed, their needs and concerns would probably suffer as majorities in each district decided on what kind of security would be provided to whom and by whom in a particular area. If middle-class homeowners were able to decide how to police drug use or prostitution in their cities, for instance, we might see greater injustices than those regularly committed against drug users and prostitutes by the public police.

The key lesson that emerges from the research on community policing and democracy is that the relationship between police forces and the communities they are meant to serve is an inherently difficult one. In recent decades efforts have been made to institute more accountability mechanisms (such as Britain's new Independent Police Complaints Commission). And numerous experiments in community policing have been undertaken, some of which have been positive for at least some sectors within communities.

One thing that would definitely improve the provision of security, including the governance of public police forces, is citizen interest and citizen involvement. Generally, citizens only take an interest in police governance — or in the broader decision-making process about whether to have a police force or some other security solution — if there is a crisis or a scandal. The 1992 police beating of Rodney King, a black motorist in Los Angeles, for example, created huge public interest in the internal workings of the Los Angeles Police Department, especially its practices in regard to race and racialized groups. A new police chief was brought in to head the LAPD and some anti-racist training was instituted. Soon enough the people of Los Angeles (and those outside LA who had followed the scandal) turned their attention to the war in Iraq and other matters, however, and police governance became relegated to small news items in the local pages of the newspapers.

Citizens of democratic countries are generally very selective in choosing what issues to learn about and discuss. The work of providing security and safety for citizens is certainly very important, and people realize that. But our attention is constantly being drawn away — by right-wing politicians as well as by police chiefs — from the everyday workings of policing to the criminal law. We are told to vote for tougher laws, for more minimum sentences, for harsher laws for young offenders, and we are told to watch judges closely to make sure they are not soft on criminals. But neither politicians nor police chiefs have any interest in involving citizens in the everyday governance of security, which in most of the developed world means basically the governance of police work. If and when police work and police governance become front-page items, if and when the absence of civilian oversight is as newsworthy as individual criminals or individual sentences — then something will begin to move on the important issue of ensuring that law enforcement practices promote rather than undermine democracy.

Police work becomes front-page news only when some blatantly corrupt or racist event is brought to light. But even if bribes and racism were eliminated from police forces, our democratic deficit would by no means be remedied. There are fundamental, structural problems that require attention. Civilian oversight may not sound very sexy, but as its absence makes clear, it is an important component of the rule of law. Citizens around the world who care about democracy, accountability and justice need to become knowledgeable about law enforcement issues and to become involved in the politics of policing — not only when there is an obvious abuse of power but on an ongoing basis. This book, I hope, will give citizens some of the information and analysis they need to do so.

27 BC The Praetorian Guard is created by Augustus. It removes cruel, weak and unpopular emperors while generally supporting just, strong and popular ones.

700 BC to modern era. Roman law provides a model legal structure for European systems, laying out definitions and principles still relevant today.

534 The Justinian Code collects existing Roman law into a simple and clear system of laws, or code.

1100 The written Charter of Liberties or Coronation Charter is proclaimed by Henry I of England.

1215 The Magna Carta Libertatum or Great Charter of Freedoms is issued, leading to the rule of constitutional law in the English-speaking world.

1689 The Glorious Revolution in England establishes a constitutional monarchy, a system in which the sovereign cannot in most instances overrule Parliament.

1776 American Declaration of Independence.

1791 First Amendment to the US Constitution puts freedom of speech on a higher plane than ordinary laws.

1789 The French Revolution results in Europe's first Declaration of Rights of Man and the Citizen.

1804 The Napoleonic Civil Code is drafted. It is still the basis of the legal systems of most countries except China and the English-speaking world.

1832 Sir Robert Peel creates the first body of uniformed constables in the United Kingdom, officers who later are known as "bobbies."

1917   The Russian Revolution leads to the creation of the Soviet Union and a one-party communist government.

1933   Adolf Hitler is named chancellor of Germany; he establishes the Third Reich, suspending most of the human rights provided by the 1919 constitution of the Weimar Republic.

The Gestapo is created as a special secret police exempt from judicial oversight.

1945-46   The Nuremberg Trials take place in Germany, the first instance of an international war crimes trial.

1948   The United Nations Universal Declaration of Human Rights is the first document to recognize human rights at the level of the whole world rather than at the national level – although the UN did not create either a world police or a world human rights court to enforce these rights.

1954   *Brown v. Board of Education of Topeka.* United States Supreme Court declares that the state laws that established separate public schools for black and white students deny black children equal educational opportunities. Many Southern schools and institutions are forcibly integrated using troops.

The KGB (Committee for State Security) is created. It is the Soviet Union's secret police, internal security and espionage organization until 1991.

1973   Chile's democratically elected president Salvador Allende is overthrown by the army, led by General Augusto Pinochet, with the US government condoning the coup.

1976   Tiananmen Square (China). Students engaged in mild protest are attacked by tanks; repression grows in China.

1990   Nelson Mandela is released from prison. Mandela then leads the transition toward multi-racial democracy in South Africa.

1992   The High Court of Australia, in its decision in the Mabo case, recognizes that the white legal fiction that Australia had been *terra nullius* (unoccupied land) before the arrival of the English is untrue and unjust.

2002   The International Criminal Court (ICC) is established in the Hague (the Netherlands), with jurisdiction over genocide, crimes against humanity and war crimes.

2009   The ICC issues an arrest warrant for Omar al-Bashir of Sudan for war crimes and crimes against humanity.

2010   In the wake of a major earthquake, thousands of troops from the UN, the US and other countries arrive in Haiti to maintain order and ensure that food aid is fairly distributed. Many inside and outside the country worry that policing and security matters will remain in foreign hands for years to come.

Notes

1 What Is the Law?

1. Walter Benjamin, "Theses on the Philosophy of History," in *Illuminations*, ed. Hannah Arendt (New York: Basic Books, 1968).

2 Kafka's Challenge

1. Franz Kafka, *The Trial* (New York: Chelsea House, 1987), 2, 4.
2. Ibid., 5.
3. The Magna Carta, in facsimile and in translation, is available at http://www.bl.uk/treasures/magnacarta/.

3 Law and Culture, Law and Justice

1. All of Mandela's speeches are available at http://www.anc.org.za/ancdocs/history/mandela/. The Rivonia speech is under "1960."

4 Who Are the Police?

1. Max Weber, "Politics as a Vocation," in *From Max Weber* (New York: Oxford University Press, 1958).
2. Hugo Fruhling, "The Impact of International Models of Policing in Latin America: The Case of Community Policing," *Policing Practice and Research* Vol. 8, No. 2 (May 2007), 125-44.
3. Michael Taussig, *Law in a Lawless Land* (Chicago: University of Chicago Press, 2003).
4. Ibid., 53.
5. Ibid., 132.
6. Ibid., 188-89.
7. Mark Button, *Private Policing* (London: Willan, 2002).

5 What Do Police Do?

1. Ronald Kessler, *The Bureau: The Secret History of the FBI* (New York: St Martin's Press, 2002); Philip Jenkins, *Using Murder:*

The Social Construction of Serial Homicide (New York: A. De Gruyter, 1994).

2. Adam Crawford and Stuart Lister, *The Use and Impact of Dispersal Orders* (Leeds: Leeds University Centre for Criminal Justice Studies, 2007).

3. Wilson, James Q. and George Kelling, "Fixing Broken Windows," *Atlantic Monthly*, February 1982, 32.

4. Richard V. Ericson, *Making Crime: A Study of Detective Work* (Toronto: University of Toronto Press, 1993); Richard V. Ericson and Kevin Haggerty, *Policing the Risk Society* (Toronto: University of Toronto Press, 1997).

6 Law's Harms

1. Julia Buxton, *The Political Economy of Narcotics* (London: Zed, 2006).

2. See Coletta Youngers and Eileen Rosin, eds., *Drugs and Democracy in Latin America: The Impact of US Policy* (Boulder: Lynne Riener, 2005).

3. Buxton, *The Political Economy of Narcotics*, 92.

4. The figures are from official government sources compiled by Buxton, *The Political Economy of Narcotics*, 107.

5. James Austin et al., "The Use of Incarceration in the United States," *Critical Criminology* Vol. 10, No. 1 (2001); B. Pettit and B. Western, "Mass Imprisonment and the Life Course: Race and Class Inequality in US Incarceration," *American Sociological Review* Vol. 69 (2004), 151-69.

7 The Politics of Policing in Democratic Societies

1. See Naomi Klein, "Police and Tasers: Hooked on Shock," February 11, 2008, http://www.naomiklein.org/articles/2008/02/police-and-tasers.

2. See "Tasers – Potentially Lethal and Easy to Abuse," press release for the report at http://www.amnesty.org/en/news-and-updates/report/tasers-potentially-lethal-and-easy-

abuse-20081216. The report, *'Less Than Lethal'? The Use Of Stun Weapons in US Law Enforcement* (Amnesty International, December 2008) is available on the same website.

3. "Taser FAQ," CBC News, available at http://www.cbc.ca/canada/story/2009/03/18/f-taser-faq.html.

4. "Tasers – Potentially Lethal and Easy to Abuse."

5. "Taser FAQ," CBC News.

6. Adam Crawford, *The Local Governance of Crime: Appeals to Community and Partnerships* (Oxford: Clarendon, 1997).

7. Mutuma Ruteere and Marie-Emmanuelle Pommerolle, "Democratizing Security or Decentralizing Repression? The Ambiguities of Community Policing in Kenya," *African Affairs* No. 102 (2003), 587-604.

8. Suzette Heald, "Controlling Crime and Corruption from Below: *Sungusungu* in Kenya," *International Relations* Vol. 21, No. 2 (2007), 183-99.

9. Numerous studies of policing and security issues in South Africa are available online at The Institute of Criminology of the University of Capetown website, http://www.uct.ac.za/faculties/law/research/criminol/

10. Les Johnston and Clifford Shearing, *Governing Security: Explorations in Policing and Justice* (London: Routledge, 2003), 114.

For Further Information

Books

Brogden, Mike and Clifford Shearing. *Policing in the New South Africa*. London: Routledge, 1992.

Crenshaw, Kimberle, ed. *Critical Race Theory: The Key Writings*. New York: New Press, 1995.

Jones, Trevor and Tim Newburn, eds. *Plural Policing: A Comparative Perspective*. New York: Routledge, 2006.

Lacey, Nicola. *State Punishment: Political Principles and Community Values*. London: Routledge, 1988.

Simon, Jonathan. *Governing Through Crime*. Oxford: Oxford University Press, 2007.

Smart, Carol. *Feminism and the Power of Law*. London: Routledge, 1989.

Websites

http://www.amnesty.org

Amnesty International has an excellent website in Arabic, French, Spanish and English, with up-to-date information about human rights and other legal issues, by country and by topic.

http://www.hrw.org

Human Rights Watch investigates abuses of state power, including many that concern criminal justice, around the world. Its reports, often based on original research, are considered authoritative.

http://web.uct.ac.za/depts/criminology

The Centre of Criminology at the University of Cape Town makes a lot of information about policing and other legal issues available through its website. The focus is on Africa but much of the content is of global value.

http://criminology.utoronto.ca:80/lib/

The Centre of Criminology at the University of Toronto has a Library and Information Service that facilitates access to research studies and materials.

Index